IRAN&
ISRAEL

MARK
HITCHCOCK

HARVEST HOUSE PUBLISHERS
EUGENE, OREGON

Cover by Left Coast Design, Portland, Oregon

Cover photo © Benjamin Haas / Shutterstock

Published in association with William K. Jensen Literary Agency, 119 Bampton Court, Eugene, Oregon 97404.

IRAN AND ISRAEL
Copyright © 2013 by Mark Hitchcock
Published by Harvest House Publishers
Eugene, Oregon 97402
www.harvesthousepublishers.com

Library of Congress Cataloging-in-Publication Data
Hitchcock, Mark, 1959-
Iran and Israel / Mark Hitchcock.
    p. cm.
ISBN 978-0-7369-5334-4 (pbk.)
ISBN 978-0-7369-5335-1 (eBook)
1. Islam—Iran. 2. Iran--Social conditions—1997- 3. Iran—Politics and government—1997- 4. Iran—Economic conditions—1997- 5. Nuclear weapons—Iran. 6. Iran—Foreign relations—Israel. 7. Israel—Foreign relations—Iran. 8. Bible—Prophecies. I. Title.
BP63.I68H58 2013
220.1'5—dc23

                                                    2012031798

Printed in the United States of America

13 14 15 16 17 18 19 20 21 / BP-CD / 10 9 8 7 6 5 4 3

To Tim LaHaye
Thank you for your friendship and encouragement.
You are a blessing to me and my family and
the body of Christ.

Contents

CHAPTER ONE   As Time Runs Out
Are We on the Road to Apocalypse? / **9**

CHAPTER TWO   Iran vs. Israel—from Shadow War to Showdown
"Accidents," Assassinations, and Attack / **35**

CHAPTER THREE   Show Me the Mahdi
An Apocalyptic, Genocidal Ideology Drives Iran / **55**

CHAPTER FOUR   Unleashing the Dogs of Terror
Hamas and Hezbollah Strike Israel / **75**

CHAPTER FIVE   What Will Happen to America?
*Bible Prophecy Is Silent About
America's Role in the End Times* / **91**

CHAPTER SIX   The Coming Middle East Peace
A Temporary Middle East Peace Is on the Horizon / **109**

CHAPTER SEVEN   The Ezekiel Prophecy
Bible Prophecy Predicts a Future Middle East War / **123**

CHAPTER EIGHT   The Times of the Signs
*Current Developments Strikingly Foreshadow
the End of Days* / **155**

CHAPTER NINE   Do Not Let Your Heart Be Troubled
Finding Peace in a World at War / **171**

APPENDIX ONE   The Persia Prophecies / **185**

APPENDIX TWO   America in Prophecy (Dr. John F. Walvoord) / **197**

APPENDIX THREE   Ezekiel 38–39 / **205**

NOTES   **211**

"A country that builds underground nuclear facilities, develops intercontinental ballistic missiles, manufactures thousands of centrifuges, and that absorbs crippling sanctions, is doing all that in order to advance...medical research...Ladies and gentlemen, if it looks like a duck, walks like a duck, and quacks like a duck, then what is it? That's right, it's a duck. But this duck is a nuclear duck. And it's time the world started calling a duck a duck."[1]

—BENJAMIN NETANYAHU

"If they arrive at military nuclear capability, at a weapon, or a demonstrated capability, or a threshold status in which they could manufacture a bomb within 60 days—they will achieve a different kind of immunity, regime immunity."[2]

—EHUD BARAK

"The single biggest danger in the Middle East today is not the risk of a six-day Israeli war with Iran. It is the risk that Western wishful nonthinking allows the mullahs of Iran to get their hands on nuclear weapons. Because I am in no doubt that they would take full advantage of such a lethal lever. We would have acquiesced in the creation of an empire of extortion. War is an evil. But sometimes a preventive war can be a lesser evil than a policy of appeasement. The people who don't yet know that are the ones still in denial about what a nuclear-armed Iran would end up costing us all. It feels like the eve of some creative destruction."[3]

—NIALL FERGUSON, *Newsweek*

CHAPTER ONE

As Time Runs Out

Are We on the Road to Apocalypse?

"It's 1938 and Iran is Germany. And Iran is racing to arm itself with atomic bombs. Believe him and stop him... This is what we must do. Everything else pales before this."[1]

Benjamin Netanyahu

"Imagine that you wake up tomorrow morning and discover that during the night, Israeli planes had conducted a bombing raid on Iran. How would your world have changed?"[2]

Gary Sick, CNN.com

A uthors Yaakov Katz and Yoaz Hendel set the scene for what we might see unfold in the near future:

The briefing room will be packed when the prime minister takes his position at the podium and asks everyone to sit down. As the young pilots stare up at their nation's leader, the prime minister will gaze right into their eyes, searching for one more confirmation that he has made the right decision.

While clearly nervous, the pilots are ready. They have been prepared for this day for the past few years, some of them from the beginning of their Israel Defense Force service. The prime minister does not have much to say.

"This is a historic day for our small nation," he will announce. "Some seventy years ago Nazi Germany tried to destroy our people, but we survived and succeeded in establishing the State of Israel. It is now up to you to ensure that we will continue to survive and live here."

Then the rabbi for the Israeli Air Force will stand up at the podium, and all of the pilots will cover their heads. Together they will say the Traveler's Prayer, a short plea to God written at the time of the Talmud, to ask that they make it to their destination and return safely.

At once, the pilots stand and salute the prime minister, the defense minister, and IAF commander. Minutes later, they climb inside their aircraft and begin lining them up along the runway.

The prime minister had actually made up his mind to attack Iran several months earlier but had waited, hoping to coordinate the operation with the White House. While the president tried to persuade Israel to back down and even threatened to cut military aid, the Israeli leader explained that he was not asking for permission. Instead, the prime minister asserted, he was doing what allies do and informing the president of his government's decision ahead of time. The Israeli cabinet had spoken: Iran's nuclear program had to be stopped.[3]

One thing is clear. If Israel launches a preemptive strike against Iran's nuclear sites, things will never be the same. Not for Israel. Not for the Middle East. Not for the world. The attack will trigger a cascade of events that could bring strong retaliation from Iran and its proxies Hezbollah and Hamas, all of whom may pound Israel with rockets and missiles. Israel could find itself fighting fierce onslaughts on the northern front, the southern front, and the home front. Such a war could spark a wider regional conflict, with Iran attacking American forces in the Persian Gulf and Saudi oil fields. The question of what America will do is unclear. Some fear that an Israeli preemptive assault could even start World War III.

No one knows the nature and extent of the immediate fallout. There will undoubtedly be many twists and turns. But is it possible that these events are part of a larger drama scripted long ago? Can we know how these events correspond to the pattern of events foretold by the ancient prophets to know where it's all headed? In the uncertain storm of the days in which we live, we all yearn to look into the darkness of the future to see what's ahead—but can we?

STRIKE THREE?

Israeli jets thundered across the Iraqi desert on June 7, 1981, shocking the world by taking out an Iraqi nuclear reactor. The mission, code-named "Operation Opera," was ordered by Prime Minister Menachem Begin to take out the French-built nuclear plant in Osirak, 18 miles south of Baghdad. In this preemptive strike, eight Israeli Air Force (IAF) F-16 fighter jets destroyed the 70-megawatt uranium-powered reactor, dropping sixteen 2000-pound bombs—14 of which made direct hits.

Twenty-six years later, on September 6, 2007, in a daring midnight strike code-named "Operation Orchard," Israeli warplanes destroyed a secret nuclear reactor in the remote Syrian desert about 20 miles west of Damascus. The world didn't even know about it until weeks later.

Twice already, in daring preemptive strikes, Israel has taken out the nuclear ambitions of its enemies. Israel has vowed that it will deliver strike three to the Iranian nuclear facilities if the world doesn't act and Iran fails to stand down in its nuclear aspirations. Israeli General Daniel Halutz was asked back on March 7, 2006, "How far would Israel go to stop Iran's nuclear program?" He calmly responded, "2000 kilometers."[4] That's the distance from Israel to Iran.

What he said in 2006 has not changed. To the contrary, Israeli resolve has hardened. Israel will go to any lengths to interrupt the Iranian nuclear machine. The Iranian centrifuges are spinning. Iran and Israel are already at war. Open conflict appears inevitable. Jeffrey Goldberg observes, "Netanyahu isn't bluffing—he is in fact counting down to the day when he will authorize a strike against a half-dozen or more Iranian nuclear sites."[5] Israel believes that it has the capacity to cause enough damage to set Iran's nuclear program back by three to five years.[6] *The New York Times* has envisioned an Israeli surgical strike by 100 planes.[7] Note also this article by D.B. Grady:

> No sane person would wish for a unilateral Israeli strike on Iranian nuclear facilities—but nor would a sane person wish for a nuclear Iran… But if intelligence suggested an impending, existential threat to Israel, it's easy to imagine F-15I fighter jets planting GBU-28 bunker-busters in Iranian nuclear sites from the Caspian Sea to the Persian Gulf. And if that happens, the real question becomes, what next?[8]

That's the question everyone is asking. What's next? Will there be an Iranian counterstrike? What will it look like? How aggressive and far-reaching will it be? What will Hezbollah and Hamas do? Will the United States be drawn into the fray? Could it trigger a larger regional war? Or even World War III?

War games conducted by the U.S. military in March

2012 concluded that an Israeli strike against Iran "would likely lead to a wider war that could include the U.S."[9] Iran has threatened to target U.S. bases if the U.S. is part of any attack against Iran, saying that American bases in the Middle East are "highly vulnerable" and can be destroyed minutes after the attack.

The U.S. conducted a two-week war game called "Internal Look" that "played out a narrative in which the United States found it was pulled into the conflict after Iranian missiles struck a Navy warship in the Persian Gulf, killing about 200 Americans."[10] In this scenario, the U.S. carried out its own strikes on Iranian nuclear facilities. "General Mattis told aides that an Israeli first strike would be likely to have dire consequences across the region and for United States forces there."[11]

Israel has also conducted its own war games, and Israel's war games concluded it could deal a crippling blow to Iran's nuclear pursuits:

> In a simulation war game featuring Israelis in senior positions, Israel loses 10 fighter jets in a strike on Iran's nuclear facilities and manages to set back the Iranian nuclear program by seven years…According to the game's premise…four independent and reliable Mossad intelligence sources indicate that Iran has begun transferring its strategic nuclear equipment to underground sites in Qom.
>
> Iran sends 1,500 tanks toward the border with Iraq and instructs Hizbullah to fire missiles

at Israel. It also launches a series of large scale
terror actions and fires missiles from Lebanon
and from its own territory at hi-tech targets in
Herzliya, succeeding in destroying Intel's headquarters. A suicide bomber kills a large number
of cadets in the IDF's hi-tech Talpiyot program.
Low-level radiation is released in Tel Aviv by a
"dirty bomb." In the war game, Israeli media
shows surprising solidarity and unity on the day
of the attack, initially sparing the government
from criticism...

Iran decides to try and drive a wedge between
Israel and the U.S. It therefore tells the U.S. it
will supply it with as much oil as it needs...its
agents blow up a car bomb in Tel Aviv and fire
a missile at an El Al jet from a ship in the Mediterranean, killing 300 people. Meanwhile, intelligence indicates that Iran's nuclear program has
been set back 7 years by the Israeli strikes.[12]

How close this simulation is to what really happens remains to be seen. Reports of a secret agreement
between Azerbaijan in Central Asia and Israel came to
light in the spring of 2012. According to these leaks, the
Azeri government has granted Israel access to eight air
bases located just 200 miles north of Iran which would
allow Israel to land and refuel fighters and bombers in
very close proximity to its targets.[13] The world views this
as one more signal that Israel and Iran are one step closer
to war and that simulation will give way to realization.

Once the dominos begin to fall, all bets are off. But it's clear that Iran's fury and revenge will be targeted against Israel, which it calls the "little Satan," and the U.S., which was dubbed the "great Satan" in 1979.

ISRAEL AND THE U.S. IN THE CROSSHAIRS

The mullah regime in Iran, according to Israeli Prime Minister Benjamin Netanyahu, poses an "existential threat" to Jewish people and their homeland. Iranian leaders continue to spew out venom against Israel that openly unmasks their evil intentions. Iran's supreme leader Ayatollah Ali Khamenei has referred to Israel as a "cancerous tumor that should be cut and will be cut."[14] Several Iranian defectors have made it clear that Khamenei is directly involved in the nuclear program. He makes the final decisions. Scientists who have defected from Iran have given differing measures of the state of Iran's nuclear development, but "they were all clear about Iran's true intentions, however: the Islamic Republic was developing the bomb so it could one day attack Israel."[15]

Alireza Forghani, a strategy specialist and staunch supporter of Supreme Leader Ayatollah Ali Khamenei, has released a detailed military plan to annihilate Israel, which he claims can be accomplished in less than nine minutes using Iranian missiles. He maintains that "Tehran is capable of annihilating Israel within less than nine minutes using its arsenal of missiles and by deploying operational combat units throughout the world."[16] He says that Iran will hit targets inside Israel, including nuclear facilities, air force bases, and civilian infrastructure. Ayatollah Khamenei has warned of a "lightning response" to any preemptive attack by Israel. He said, "Should they take any wrong step, any inappropriate move, it will fall on their heads like lightning."[17]

But Israel is not alone as the focus of Iranian malice. For the Iranian regime, the U.S. is part of its plan for annihilation. Ayatollah Khamenei stated, "In light of the realization of the divine promise by almighty God, the Zionists and the Great Satan [America] will soon be defeated." Some Israeli officials claim that Iran is working to develop a long-range missile capable of reaching the United States. Americans believe the threat posed by Iran is great. A CNN poll found that fear of Iran in the U.S. "has surpassed fear of the Soviet Union during one of the Cold War's most dangerous years."[18] The poll revealed that 81 percent of Americans believe Iran is a "very serious" or "moderately serious" threat, with 48 percent calling it "very serious."[19] Eighty-four percent of Americans believe Iran is developing nuclear weapons, and 71 percent believe they already have the bomb.[20]

Despite repeated, drawn-out diplomatic efforts and rounds and rounds of sanctions, Iran has steadfastly clung to its right to a nuclear program that the entire world knows is focused on developing the bomb. Iranian President Mahmoud Ahmadinejad has said, "The train of the Iranian nation is without brakes and a rear gear…We dismantled the reverse gear and brakes of the train and threw them away some time ago."[21] He also said, "Nuclear energy is our right, and we will resist until this right is fully realized." As Ehud Barak notes, "This is not about some abstract concept, but a genuine concern. The Iranians are, after all, a nation whose leaders have set themselves a strategic goal of wiping Israel off the map." Barak has repeatedly warned that time is "urgently running out."[22] It seems to have already run out. The drums of war are pounding. Zero hour has arrived. Israel will unleash a unilateral, preemptive strike to diminish Iran's nuclear charge.

The Israel vs. Iran showdown has given rise to a new measure of the probability that the U.S. or Israel will strike Iran. It's sponsored by *The Atlantic* and is called the "Iran War Dial."

The Dial is set by a panel of esteemed experts who periodically predict the odds of conflict. Each panelist predicts the percentage chance of war, and then the scores are averaged to come up with the chance of war, thus, the "Iran War Dial."[23] The hands on the Dial may be near midnight. The moment of truth has arrived.

"Strait" Talk about Oil and Global Recession

One nightmare consequence of war with Iran is the threat of major disruption of oil supplies. Iran has threatened to close the Strait of Hormuz and shut off the spigot of Persian Gulf oil. Parviz Sarvari, a member of the Iranian Parliament's National Security Committee, said, "Soon we will hold a military maneuver on how to close the Strait of Hormuz. If the world wants to make the region insecure, we will make the world insecure."[24]

The Strait of Hormuz is a narrow strait, and it's the only sea passage to the open ocean for the Persian Gulf nations. The strait is located between Iran and the United Arab Emirates. It's 21 miles wide at its narrowest point, but it has only two one-mile wide channels for sea traffic. These two travel channels are separated by a two-mile buffer zone.

About 17 million barrels of oil a day navigate their way through the Strait of Hormuz. This represents about 20 percent of the world's total daily oil supply and about 40 percent of the world's seaborne oil trade. Supplies from Saudi Arabia, Kuwait, Iraq, and Iran must pass through this narrow strait. Remember that these four nations have almost two-thirds of the world's proven oil reserves. And the oil that travels through that narrow waterway represents almost all of the world's spare capacity.

This means that Iran is the daily gatekeeper for 20 percent of the world's daily oil supply. Iran overlooks the strategic world oil chokepoint on the Strait of Hormuz. Experts believe that Iran already has a strategic plan in place to execute suicide attacks on U.S. military vessels in the Persian Gulf. Iran's elite Revolutionary Guards have conducted war games in the Strait of Hormuz. Iranian ships in the strait are being equipped with shorter-range missiles.

Also, the narrow strait could easily be shut down simply by the placement of a few sea mines in the narrow lanes. Iran currently possesses EM-53 bottom-tethered mines that it purchased from China in the 1990s. The navy says that it could take months to locate and remove these

mines. And just think what would happen if Iran sunk a
couple of full oil supertankers in the strait. It would be
disastrous. The environmental effects would be far-
reaching, and oil prices would skyrocket overnight. With
20 percent of the world's oil supply cut off indefinitely,
the already shaky world economy could plunge into the
financial abyss. Global recession would inevitably result.
The fear alone of an Israeli attack on Iran raised the price
for a gallon of gas by at least 25 cents according to experts.
Prices would soar in the event of an actual attack. On
average, 14 crude oil tankers pass through the strait each
day, carrying an estimated 17 million barrels, more than
a third of the world's seaborne oil shipments.[25] A study
of nearly 800 institutional investors conducted by the
Economist Intelligence Unit found the primary risk to
the global economic recovery is the threat of an oil price
spike, which is primarily linked to tensions over Iran's
nuclear program.

One article puts it this way:

> Assuming a military confrontation between
> Iran, Israel and the U.S.—specifically, an attack
> on Iran's nuclear facilities—does take place, the
> EIU forecasts a "severe oil price spike amount-
> ing to a 30-50 percent jump in prices in a matter
> of days or weeks, halting the global economic
> recovery and threatening another recession."[26]

The U.S. has clearly said that any attempt by Iran to close the strait or lay mines is an "act of war," according to Vice Admiral Mark Fox.[27] Based on Iranian threats of retaliatory actions, the United States has "deployed a second aircraft carrier task force in the Arabian Sea close to the Straits and doubled the number of minesweepers based inside the Persian Gulf at Bahrain from four to eight. The U.S. has also fielded an undisclosed number of F-22 Raptor stealth fighters-bombers to a base in the same general area."[28] The U.S. Fifth Fleet is based in Bahrain. Preparations must be carefully made for any and every eventuality if and when Israel launches a preemptive strike.

IT WILL BE MUCH HARDER THIS TIME

The Israeli success in destroying the nuclear facilities in Iraq and Syria will be much more difficult, if not impossible, to replicate. Iran is a nation of about 80 million people inhabiting 1.65 million square kilometers and the nuclear targets in Iran are 1000 miles from Israel. It is the eighteenth largest country in the world in size, and the seventeenth largest in population.

Also, Iran's nuclear program is not concentrated in one location or even one facility. It's spread out in seven places.

Iran's Seven Key Nuclear Facilities

Bushehr Nuclear Power Plant
This Russian-built nuclear reactor began producing electricity in 2010.

Arak Heavy Water Reactor

This is still under construction, but it will eventually produce weapons-grade plutonium.

Natanz Enrichment Facility

As Iran's main enrichment center, it is located partly underground, and it can hold up to 50,000 centrifuges and currently has almost 10,000 spinning.

Isfahan Nuclear Technology Center

Built in 2006, it converts yellowcake to uranium hexafluoride.

Tehran Nuclear Research Center

This center is made up of labs where nuclear research is conducted.

Bandar Abbas Uranium Production Plant

This plant processes uranium ore.

Fordo Uranium Enrichment Plant

Buried 300 feet underneath a mountain next to a military complex, this site was kept secret until it was identified by Western intelligence agencies in September 2009. Iran finally had to acknowledge the existence of the facility at that time. The facility, which is a hardened tunnel, is protected by air defense missiles and the Iranian Revolutionary Guard. It can hold up to 3000 centrifuges.

A Daunting Task

Taking out Iran's nuclear facilities or even stunting their growth for a few years is a daunting task. "The Natanz complex consists of two large halls, roughly 300,000 square feet each, dug somewhere between eight and twenty-three feet below ground and covered with several layers of concrete and metal. The walls of each hall are estimated to be two feet thick."[29]

At Iran's Fordo site near Iran's holy city of Qom, centrifuges are churning out uranium enriched to over 20 percent, which "can be turned into fissile warhead material faster and with less work."[30] This level of enrichment is not necessary for industrial use. The heavily fortified Fordo facility is buried 300 feet under a mountain, which means that inflicting significant damage will be difficult. Ehud Barak has stated that the facility is "immune to standard bombs."[31] In spite of the daunting challenges, Israel will be forced to strike and inflict whatever damage possible unless there is some drastic change.

The choice for Israel is quickly narrowing to two options: Either they carry out the bombing, or they suffer the bomb. And both Israel and the United States have said forcefully and repeatedly that they will not allow Iran to get the bomb. According to reports from the International Atomic Energy Agency, Iran is dead set on crossing the nuclear finish line:

> Iran has significantly stepped up its output of low-enriched uranium and total production in

the last five years would be enough for at least five nuclear weapons if refined much further… Iran has produced almost 6.2 tons of uranium enriched to a level of 3.5 percent since it began the work in 2007—some of which has subsequently been further processed into higher-grade material. This is nearly 750 kg more than in the previous IAEA report issued in February, and ISIS said Iran's monthly production had risen by roughly a third. This total amount of 3.5 percent low enriched uranium hexafluoride, if further enriched to weapon grade, is enough to make over five nuclear weapons.[32]

So, barring some unforeseen, unimaginable walk-back by Iran, the only option for Israel is bombing. Michael Oren, Israeli Ambassador to the U.S., framed the issue succinctly: "America, a big country, has a big window, looks out that window and sees the Middle East far away; Israel, a small country with a very small window, we look out that window and we see Iran in our backyard."[33] That's the issue. A nuclear Iran is not an option for Israel.

If Iran goes nuclear, it could transfer a nuclear device to one of its terrorist proxies to be detonated in Israel or the United States. A nuclear Iran would also trigger a nuclear arms race in the world's most volatile region. As Israeli Defense Minister Ehud Barak says, "The moment Iran goes nuclear, other countries in the region will feel compelled to do the same. The Saudi Arabians have told the Americans as much, and one can think of both

Turkey and Egypt in this context, not to mention the
danger that weapons-grade materials will leak out to terror groups." Henry Kissinger also sounds the alarm about
Iran's drive to the nuclear finish line: "If Iran is allowed
to produce nuclear weapons, the genie will be out of
the bottle, and the whole world will be in grave danger."
Imagine terrorist organizations in the Middle East getting their hands on a nuclear weapon or even radioactive
material to make a "dirty bomb." A nuclear-armed Iran
will also push the most militant factions within Hezbollah and other Iranian surrogates to step up their aggres-
sion and take greater risks. [34]

THE VOICE OF THE PROPHETS

Of course, all the recent developments with Israel and
Iran present formidable economic, political, and military
challenges for the U.S., Israel, and other Western nations.
A great deal of diplomatic capital has been expended.
There are no easy solutions. Confrontation looms.

But could the rise of Iran and its stance toward Israel
have even greater significance? Could events we are witnessing today be preparing the way for the fulfillment
of Bible prophecy? Only God knows for sure, but many
signs point in that direction. As alarming as current
events are in the Middle East, they shouldn't be surprising in light of the end-time prophecies of the Bible.

The biblical prophecy in Ezekiel 38–39, written about
2600 years ago, tells us that a great horde of nations will
invade Israel in the last days while Israel is at rest in her

own land. The leader of this invasion will apparently be Russia, and one of the main allies in this confederation of nations, according to Ezekiel 38:5, is Persia—the modern nation of Iran. Russia has risen to world prominence in the last century, and it has experienced a great resurgence in the last decade. Iran is now world public enemy number one and an avowed anti-Semitic state, which has pledged to "wipe Israel off the map."

I want to be clear that I don't believe the current crisis in Iran and the Middle East is the direct fulfillment of any biblical prophecy. However, it is an ominous development that strikingly foreshadows what the Bible predicts. It is a significant signpost that I believe points toward the fulfillment of the great prophecy of Ezekiel 38–39. In the surging events in the Middle East, we can hear the pounding of prophetic hoofbeats.

Israel's strike against Iran's nuclear facilities will probably unleash a vicious backlash. Dominos will begin to fall. No one knows for sure how they will fall, or how many will fall, but we know some will fall. We also know that some consequences will develop immediately, while others may slowly smolder. But one thing is clear: Ahmadinejad and the Iranian mullahs already harbor a devilish hatred for the U.S. and Israel. Just think how they would go off if Israel stalled their nuclear program. Any military action by the U.S. or Israel (or both) against Iran would undoubtedly plant seeds of vengeful animosity in Iran that could later erupt in the fulfillment of the biblical prophecy in Ezekiel 38–39. We may be witnessing the stage-setting for this incredible prophecy right now! The pieces of Ezekiel's prophetic puzzle seem to be coming together. It appears that the end-time stage is being set right before our eyes.

In the Theater of World Events

The setting of the world stage for future, end-time events can be graphically illustrated by picturing a theater where preparations are made for a production. Suppose a Shakespearean actor enters a theater one evening, not knowing what masterpiece of Shakespeare is to be presented. Before the curtain goes up, he is taken behind the scenes.

On stage is a castle with fortifications looking out over a wooded countryside. At once he knows that he will not see *Othello*, which is set in Venice, nor *Julius Caesar*, which begins with a street scene in Rome. He knows that he will not see *Macbeth*, for even though a castle scene does take place in *Macbeth*, the play opens not with the castle but with witches gathered around their cauldron. Finally, our drama critic notices two soldiers with shields bearing the arms of the king of Denmark. He sees two other actors dressed up as a king and a queen and one actor who is supposed to be a ghost. Now no one has to tell the critic what he will see, for he knows it will be *Hamlet*.

In the same way today, God's people sit in the theater of world events awaiting the curtain call of God's apocalyptic drama. We don't know when the play will begin, but like the drama critic, we know much more about it

than most. Many stare at the future as a huge curtain.
For them, the future is veiled—they have no idea of the
plan of God. And they can't see behind the curtain where
Act One is being set. But as believers, we see behind the
scenes. While it is true that we don't know the moment
when the play will begin, we do know the play itself—the
main characters and events—and can sense it beginning
as we see the actors starting to take their proper places on
the great world stage.[35]

The Jewish people are back in their ancient homeland after being scattered to 70 countries for almost 2000
years. They are surrounded by a sea of enemies, just as
Scripture predicted. Iran has risen to power as both the
dominant military power in the Middle East and the
world's largest state sponsor of terror. At the same time,
the Russian bear has roared out of hibernation to reassert
its influence and lend its support to the Iranian regime.
Rolling revolutions in the Arab world have created an
uncertain future. The world economy is teetering on the
brink of recession or even worse. People everywhere are
crying out for peace in the Middle East.

Behind all of this looms the ancient prophecy of Ezekiel 38–39, which predicts that Iran (ancient Persia) will
be a key player in the end times and that Iran will join a
confederacy of other nations to attack Israel. What we see
happening appears to point toward the fulfillment of this
great prophecy.

Over twenty years ago, prophecy scholar Dr. John
Walvoord noted that the first key to the Armageddon
countdown is that "the Middle East must become the

number one crisis in the world."[36] There's no doubt that
the Middle East is the number one hot spot in the world.
That piece of the prophetic puzzle is now firmly in place.

What will happen next? Where's it all headed? Are
there any answers? Can we know the future? What is
Russia's role in the end times? What does the Bible say
about the future of the Middle East? Will Iran try to shut
off the Strait of Hormuz, causing panic on world oil markets? How high will oil go? What will happen to the
world economy? Will Iran attack U.S. ships in the Persian
Gulf, drawing the U.S. into another war? Will the Middle East go up in the flames of a regional war? What will
Russia do? What are the final events of history? Is there
any way to know what the future holds? Is there a word
of comfort or a warning of cataclysm?

This is a book about current events, but more particu-
larly, it is about how current events point toward what's
coming in the future. Before we get too deep into the
details of what's transpiring in the Middle East and where
it's all headed, I believe it's important to get our bear-
ings by understanding the overall prophetic scenario presented in Scripture. To accomplish this, let's begin with
the time we are in today—a time known as the church
age—and then progress briefly through a few key end-
time events.

THE CURRENT CHURCH AGE

The current time period is known as the church age,
when all who come to faith in Jesus Christ are being

formed into one body with the Lord Jesus Christ as the head. As we approach the home stretch of the church age, the Jewish people have been regathered to their land. The reestablishment of the nation of Israel in the Middle East was necessary to start the calendar of end-time events because almost every end-time prophecy hinges on the existence of Israel as a nation. Since its miraculous birth, Israel has been threatened with extinction, yet it has survived in the middle of a sea of enemies.

THE GREAT ESCAPE

Someday, maybe very soon, the world will be shocked by the fulfillment of an event called *the rapture of the church*—the sudden removal of every Christian from the world (1 Thessalonians 4:13-18). This next event on God's prophetic calendar will fulfill the promise of Christ to His disciples when He said, "I will come again and receive you to Myself, that where I am, there you may be also" (John 14:3). At that time, Christians who have died will be resurrected, and every true Christian living in the world will be suddenly removed to heaven without experiencing death. Together they will meet the Lord in the air and go with Him back up to heaven to return with Him back to earth at least seven years later at His Second Coming. (Read John 14:1-3; 1 Corinthians 15:50-58; 1 Thessalonians 4:13-18.) The disappearance of millions of Christians will deepen the problems the world is facing today and plunge the world, at least temporarily, into chaos.

THE REVIVAL OF THE ROMAN EMPIRE
AND THE RISE OF ANTICHRIST

Out of the chaos produced by the rapture, a group of ten leaders, or what we might call the "Group of Ten," will rise from a reunited or revived Roman Empire centered in Europe. The Group of Ten is symbolized by the ten horns of Daniel 7:7 and the similar description of the end-time government in Revelation 13:1. This alliance or confederacy of ten leaders and the nations they represent constitutes a revival of the Roman Empire and the beginning of the final stage of the fourth beast in Daniel 7.

This power bloc will evidently include European countries and possibly nations in western Asia, northern Asia, and Africa. This group of ten leaders will control ten or more of the nations and geographic areas from the ancient Roman Empire. The Group of Ten will rise to power in the aftermath of the rapture because the world will be looking to someone to bring stability and security. This will be temporarily accomplished in a seven-year covenant of peace and protection with Israel that will bring peace to the Middle East.

From the many diplomats, negotiators, and leaders involved in the Middle East, one new international leader will emerge from Europe alongside the Group of Ten to superimpose a peace settlement on Israel and her neighbors. This man who will eventually take control of the revived Roman Empire and eventually the world is known as the Antichrist. His initial victory in international diplomacy will bring an era of false peace, a move toward disarmament, and a major push for a new world economic system. Without a forced peace, the disruption of the West's oil supply and an escalation in terrorism will threaten to bring Western civilization to its knees. The signing of this peace treaty will begin the final seven-year time of Tribulation.

THE COMING MIDDLE EAST WAR

Prophecy indicates that Israel will not be destroyed by war but will eventually be forced to accept an outside settlement at the peace table and be betrayed by the final world ruler, the Antichrist. While Israel is enjoying its peace under the guaranteed security treaty with the Antichrist, Russia and a group of Islamic allies, including Iran, will attempt a final bid for power in the Middle East, but their armies will be supernaturally destroyed in the land of Israel (Ezekiel 38–39). At this point, the balance of power will swing decisively to the world's new strongman.

THE THREE-AND-A-HALF-YEAR WORLD EMPIRE OF ANTICHRIST

As Satan's man of the hour, the Antichrist will break his covenant with Israel and attempt to destroy the Jewish people. The last half of the seven-year Tribulation, the Antichrist will rule the world politically, economically, and religiously. The entire world will give allegiance to him or suffer persecution and death (Revelation 13). In

the custom of the Roman emperors, he will deify himself
and command the worship of the world.

THE ROAD TO ARMAGEDDON

The time of Tribulation will climax with a world war
of unparalleled proportions. Hundreds of millions of
men will be involved in a gigantic world power struggle
centered in Israel (Revelation 14:19-20; 16:12-16; 19:19-
21). The tiny land of Israel will become the stage for the
greatest war of history. This war is not the same as the
Battle of Gog and Magog described in Ezekiel 38–39 that
will occur more than three and a half years earlier.

Great armies from all over the world will flood to
Israel for one final conflagration. Locked in this deadly
struggle, millions will perish in the greatest war of all history. The Bible calls this final conflict the War or Campaign of Armageddon. The word *Armageddon* comes
from the Hebrew word *Har-mageddon* (mount Megiddo)
which refers to a small hill in northern Israel that overlooks the expansive Valley of Megiddo where the troops
will muster.

Before the war is finally finished and the victor
declared, Jesus Christ will return to earth in power and
glory from heaven. His coming will be accompanied by
millions of angels and raptured Christians. It is vividly
described in Revelation 19:11-21. Coming as the King of
kings and Lord of lords, He will judge the world, destroy
the gathered armies, and usher in His own kingdom of

peace, prosperity, and righteousness on earth that will last for 1000 years (Revelation 20:1-6).

As we will see, the Bible doesn't answer every question we have or give us every detail about the future, but it does provide the template of where we're headed. The Bible is a revelation of the past, present, and future—not just of individuals but also of nations and the movements of history. It is the prism through which we can see what's coming and make sense of what's happening today. Let's begin our examination of current events and the history leading up to them through this prism and discover what it tells us about the present conflict and where it's ultimately headed.

CHAPTER TWO

Iran vs. Israel—
from Shadow War to Showdown

"Accidents," Assassinations, and Attack

*"Nobody wants to go in the direction of a
military strike... The more interesting question
is not whether it happens but how."*[1]

Matthew Kroenig, Stanton Nuclear Security Fellow
at the Council on Foreign Relations

"The hour is getting late. Very late."[2]

Benjamin Netanyahu, Prime Minister of Israel

The headlines tell the sobering story:

- "Will Israel Attack Iran?" *The New York Times*
  (January 31, 2012).

- "If Israel Bombs Iran: Forecasting the Next 24 Hours," *Yahoo News* (March 19, 2012).

- "U.S. War Game Sees Peril of Israeli Strike Against Iran," *The New York Times* (March 19, 2012).

- "Russia's Stake in Syria and Iran," *Wall Street Journal* (March 18, 2012).

- "Russia Again Warns West And Israel Not To Attack Iran," *International Business Times* (March 20, 2012).

- "U.S. Navy Head: Iran Strait 'Keeps Me Awake at Night,'" *The Jerusalem Post* (January 10, 2012).

- "Israel Super-Ready to Attack Iran if Needed," *The Jerusalem Post* (May 6, 2012).

- "Can Israel Stop Iran's Nuke Effort?" *Time* (February 6, 2012).

- "Thunder will Fall on Israel if it Attacks Iran," *Yahoo.com* (June 3, 2012).

The war between Israel and Iran has begun. The Middle East is at war. Israel and Iran have been at war since the founding of the Islamic Republic of Iran in 1979. That date marked the beginning of Iran as the world's number one supporter of terror, and it was the start of its direct opposition to the state of Israel. The rhetoric from

Iran has been ratcheted up since the mullah regime took the reins of power.

Many believe that the trouble between Iran and Israel began with the election of Mahmoud Ahmadinejad and his call for Israel to be "wiped off the map." But he was simply echoing what the Ayatollah Khomeini had said repeatedly decades earlier.

The P5+1 nations (the five permanent members of the U.N. Security Council plus Germany) have tried diplomacy for over nine years, and round after round of sanctions have been slowly tightened like a noose since 2006. Nevertheless, these sustained efforts have failed miserably. Iran has worked the "talk and build" strategy to perfection. They have delayed, stalled, and played for time. They tease the West with overtures of a possible diplomatic solution while the underground nuclear facilities are expanded and reinforced and while the centrifuges continue to spin. Iran's diplomatic dance has bought precious time for it to advance its nuclear ambitions, but the point of no return has arrived.

IRAN AND ISRAEL PRE-1978

Israeli Prime Minister Benjamin Netanyahu (often referred to as "Bibi" for short) related an interesting story to *Time* in May 2012 concerning the advice of his father:

> "My father gave me two pieces of advice when
> I went into politics," Bibi recalls. "Never touch

money, and don't use ad hominem attacks on
people. But when I became Prime Minister, I
asked him, 'What attributes does one need to
lead a country?' He was older then, and he asked
me, 'What do you think?' I said, 'You need con-
victions and courage and the ability to act.' He
said, 'You need that for anything.' He then said,
'What you need to lead a country is education,'
and by that he meant an understanding of history, the knowledge to be able to put things in
perspective."[3]

I like the counsel by Benjamin Netanyahu's father.
Every leader needs a sense of perspective—an understanding of history. The same is true when it comes to the
face-off between Israel and Iran. It's important to have a
sense of historical perspective. We have to keep in mind
that relations between Iran and Israel haven't always been
this way. Until 1978 and the Islamic revolution, Iran was
actually friendly toward Israel.

Reaching much further back, in about 538 BC, the
Persian king Cyrus the Great was a generous benefac-
tor of the Jewish people, allowing them to return to their
ancient homeland to rebuild the temple. (For more about
Cyrus and the biblical prophecies dealing with ancient
Persia, see appendix 1.) Iran's ancient predecessor, the
mighty Persian Empire, was a benevolent friend of the
Jewish people and was used by God to bless them. It's
tragic that the current leadership of Iran, which traces its
heritage back to Cyrus, now denies the Jewish claim to

the land of Israel and wants to wipe them off the face of the earth.

Fast-forwarding to the twentieth century, Iran was still a friend of Israel after the establishment of the modern state of Israel in 1948 when the Arab nations surrounding Israel mounted a campaign to drive the Jews into the sea. However, the Iranians, who are Persians, not Arabs, and who speak Farsi, not Arabic, adopted a much more positive view toward the Jewish state, as Yaakov Katz and Yoaz Hendel observe:

> On the surface, it is not obvious that Israel and Iran are enemies. The countries do not share a border, but they do share a rich history as two of the only non-Arab countries in the greater Middle East. Diplomatic ties between Israel and Iran were initiated immediately after the establishment of the Jewish state in 1948 under Israel's first prime minister, David Ben-Gurion, and lasted until Ayatollah Ruhollah Khomeini came to power in 1979, turning Iran from one of Israel's closest friends into its fiercest enemy. Israel's undeclared war with Iran began in the 1980s, when Iran founded Hezbollah; it has grown to even greater proportions since the Second Lebanon War in 2006, as have Hamas and Islamic Jihad in the Gaza Strip, also with Iranian assistance."[4]

Until 1978, Iran was actually a trusted ally of Israel. But all changed suddenly and dramatically when the Iranian revolution broke loose and the Shah of Iran was deposed. The theocracy that replaced the Shah was under the control of Ayatollah Khomeini, who turned the nation against the U.S. (the great Satan) and Israel (the little Satan). Iran's "shadow war" with Israel began in 1979. Iran joined the chorus of Arab nations who deny the right of Israel to exist. As long as Israel is in the land, they will never cease in their drive to destroy her. Twenty-five years after the Iranian revolution, the posture of Iran toward the U.S. and Israel has hardened and become much more dangerous with the outing of Iran's nuclear program in 2003.

Consider the following chart:

KEY DATES IN IRAN'S HISTORY	
550 BC	Cyrus the Great rose to power over the Medo-Persian Empire.
539 BC	Medo-Persians overthrew the city of Babylon, just as Daniel predicted in Daniel 5.
538 BC	King Cyrus allowed the Jewish people to return to Israel, ending the 70-year Babylonian captivity. Isn't it ironic that the same nation God used to allow the Jewish people to return to their national homeland over 2500 years ago is now denying their right to that land and wants to wipe them off the map?
480–473 BC	Esther married King Xerxes, and the story in the book of Esther unfolded in Persia.
444 BC	King Artaxerxes allowed Nehemiah to return to Israel to rebuild the walls of Jerusalem and restore the city.

334–331 BC	Persia was overwhelmed by Alexander the Great in a series of crushing defeats, as predicted in Daniel 8.
March 21, 1935	The name Persia was changed to Iran.
1978–79	Ayatollah Ruhollah Khomeini led the Islamic Revolution in Iran.
April 1, 1979	The name of Iran was changed to Islamic Republic of Iran.
November 4, 1979	A U.S. embassy in Tehran was seized, and 52 hostages were taken. The crisis lasted 444 days.
1982	Iran founded Hezbollah in Lebanon.
1987	Iran acquired nuclear centrifuge technology from Dr. Abdul Qadeer Khan, a renegade Pakistani engineer.
January 1995	Russia signed an $800 million nuclear plant deal with Iran to complete the nuclear plant at Bushehr.
November 2004	Iran agreed to suspend uranium enrichment.
August 2005	Mahmoud Ahmadinejad won the Iranian presidential election in June and was installed as the president of Iran in August.
January 9, 2006	Iran rebuffed European diplomatic efforts and resumed uranium production at its plant in Natanz, claiming that its only intention was to make reactor fuel to generate electricity.
March 29, 2006	The UN Security Council unanimously approved a statement demanding Iran suspend uranium enrichment.
April 9, 2006	Iran officially announced that it had begun enriching uranium.

June 2009	Mahmoud Ahmadinejad is reelected as the president of Iran.
2009–2012	Rounds of sanctions and talks are conducted.
2012	Talk of an Israeli strike against Iran escalates amid renewed negotiations and strengthened sanctions.

QUEST FOR THE BOMB

Iran's nuclear quest began in the late 1980s, when Abdul Qadeer Khan, a renegade Pakistani nuclear engineer, sold nuclear enrichment technology to Iran. Since that time, Iran has been carrying out a clandestine nuclear weapons program, one that is closely tied to national pride. It's even on full display on the Iranian currency (the rial). The Iranian 50,000-rial banknote has the nuclear symbol on its reverse side. It's like saying, "In Nukes We Trust." What does this tell us about Iran? The nuclear pursuit is now so deeply ingrained in the Iranian psyche that it's an integral part of their national pride. To surrender this right would be the ultimate humiliation.

Iran's drive for the nuclear finish line is veiled by contradictory messages. Ayatollah Khamanei issued a fatwa in 2004 declaring that Islam forbids the development or use of nuclear weapons. But it seems that he was either being less than truthful or that he has changed his mind because Iran is enriching uranium to a level beyond what is needed for civilian use.

As it presses toward its nuclear goal, Iran remains firmly dedicated to annihilating Israel. In May 2012, Major General Hassan Firouzabadi, Iran's military chief of staff, said, "The Iranian nation is standing for its cause and that is the full annihilation of Israel."[5] Ayatollah Khamenei said, "In the future too, we will support and help everyone who opposes the Zionist regime. The Zionist regime is a real cancerous tumor that should be cut and will be cut, God willing."[6] It's difficult to negotiate in good faith with a regime that holds these venomous views.

Cyber Attack

One linchpin in the ongoing shadow war being waged against Iran is computer viruses unleashed by Israel against Iran's nuclear facilities. It began with the Stuxnet worm attack in the summer of 2010 against Iran's Natanz facility. The Stuxnet worm is a piece of malware that disabled Iranian centrifuges used to enrich uranium. While it's difficult to know the full extent of the damage, the attack reportedly set Iran's nuclear program back months. The cyber security firm Symantec estimated that more than thirty thousand computer systems were affected in Iran.

The cyber attacks against Iran were also directed against its oil industry. In April 2012, "A voracious virus attack has hit computers running key parts of Iran's oil sector, forcing authorities to unplug its main oil export

terminal from the Internet and to set up a cyber crisis team."[7] The attack struck Iran's principal oil terminal
on Kharg Island, which handles 90 percent of Iran's oil
imports.[8] This hit at the very heart of Iranian commerce.
Iran is "OPEC's second-biggest exporter, after Saudi Arabia, and relies on crude sales for 80 percent of its foreign currency and for more than half of its government
finances."[9]

One article fleshes out one particular cyber attack:

> Another serious cyber attack launched by Israel
> and the U.S. is known as "Flame." Flame,
> also known as sKyWIper, is a veritable "tool-
> kit" of cyber-spying programs that is capable
> of remotely taking screenshots while the com-
> puter user works, recording audio conversa-
> tions through the computer's own microphone,
> intercepting keyboard inputs and wiping data,
> among other sophisticated capabilities, accord-
> ing to cyber-security experts. The code has been
> active for two years and has infected dozens of
> computers throughout the Middle East, mostly
> in Iran. Three cyber-security firms, both in the
> U.S. and abroad, that have begun to analyze
> Flame said the code is unprecedented in com-
> plexity and, due to its sheer sophistication, was
> most likely developed by a hacking team work-
> ing under the direction of a nation-state.[10]

Another article indicates how the Flame cyber assaults against Iran and other nations are continuing:

> *The Washington Post* reports, citing sources, that Flame was the brainchild of the U.S. National Security Agency, the Central Intelligence Agency, and Israel's military. The focus of the malware was to surreptitiously map and monitor Iran's networks to deliver sustained intelligence to the government organizations. That information could then be used for other attacks. "This is about preparing the battlefield for another type of covert action," an intelligence official told *The Washington Post*. "Cyber-collection against the Iranian program is way further down the road than this." The source went on to tell the Post that Israel and the U.S. are still conducting a cyberassault on Iran. Flame was discovered last month, but had been in operation since 2010. Kaspersky, which first noted the virus, said that it appeared to be "state-sponsored," but at the time stopped short of saying it came from the U.S. and Israel. Flame's main charge, according to security experts, was to steal information about targeted systems and stored files, as well as information on the computer display and audio conversations. Iran was the central target for the virus, but it also impacted machines in the West Bank, Syria, and other Middle East countries, as well as Sudan. The U.S. and Israel developed

and carried out the Flame virus attacks on Iran, according to a new report. [11]

In addition to the lethal computer viruses that have penetrated Iran's computer system, the Iranian nuclear program has suffered several other strange mishaps and disasters. In April 2006, two transformers blew up and fifty centrifuges were ruined during the first attempt to enrich uranium at the Natanz site. It was reported that the raw materials had been "tampered with." Also, "between January 2006 and July 2007, three airplanes belonging to Iran's Revolutionary Guards crashed under mysterious circumstances. Some reports said the planes had simply 'stopped working.'"[12] *The New York Times* reported, "In January 2007, several insulation units in the connecting fixtures of the centrifuges, which were purchased from a middleman on the black market in Eastern Europe, turned out to be flawed and unusable. Iran concluded that some of the merchants were actually straw companies that were set up to outfit the Iranian nuclear effort with faulty parts."[13]

Iran is not taking all this lying down. In response to the string of cyber attacks, Iran has been busily working to acquire the technical know-how to launch its own crippling cyber attack against the United States and its allies. Iran has invested the equivalent of more than $1 billion to bolster its cyber capabilities. Ilan Berman, vice president of the American Foreign Policy Council, said, "For the Iranian regime the conclusion is clear. War with the West, at least on the cyber front, has been joined, and the Iranian regime is mobilizing in response." How effective any Iranian cyber counterstrike could be remains to be seen, but they are working feverishly to wreak any havoc they can.

THE DEAD SCIENTISTS SOCIETY

The shadow war and covert operations between Israel and Iran has been especially devastating for top Iranian scientists. One by one they have suffered assassinations at the hands of Israeli operatives. Here's a brief list of the main targets.

January 2007	Dr. Ardeshir Husseinpour, a 44-year-old nuclear scientist working at Iran's Isfahan plant died under mysterious circumstances.
January 2010	Professor Masoud Ali-Mohammadi, a scholar at Tehran University, was assassinated by a booby-trapped motorbike in the Iranian capital.
November 2010	Majid Shahriari, an Iranian scientist was killed, and Fereydoun Abbasi-Davani, the current head of the Atomic Energy Organization of Iran, was wounded when limpet (magnet) mines were attached to their cars by motorcyclists who quickly sped away.
July 2011	A nuclear physicist was ambushed as he sat in his car outside his house. A biker shot him dead through the car window.

November 2011	A huge explosion rocked a Revolutionary Guards base 30 miles west of Tehran.
January 11, 2012	An unknown motorcyclist attached a limpet mine to the car of Iranian nuclear scientist Mostafa Ahmadi Roshan during the morning rush hour near the college building of Allameh Tabatebaei University in Iran. He was killed immediately.

Nevertheless, in spite of Israel's sustained attacks on computers and scientists, Iran has not budged. Apparently, Iranian resolve has grown stronger and more determined.

Many believe that Iran can be allowed to possess nuclear weapons and can be contained. Those who favor containment point to how the United States and the Soviet Union were able to practice restraint for several decades. But there are serious differences between the two situations. "Moscow and Washington are 5,000 miles apart. If they were 900 miles apart (as Tehran and Jerusalem are), there probably would have been a nuclear war at some point in the last 50 years. It takes a half hour for an ICBM [intercontinental ballistic missile] to fly from Moscow to Washington; that's barely enough time for the president to decide what to do if a blip on the radar screen suggests an enemy attack is underway. It takes about five minutes for a short-range missile to fly from Tehran to Israel. That's probably not enough time."[14]

OUT OF THE SHADOWS

The shadow war appears to be quickly progressing from the shadows to the sunlight. The "accidents," assassinations, and cyber warfare that have marked the shadow war have failed to stop the Iranian nuclear train. Iran's nuclear program has been outed and is quickly approaching the point of no return.

> Iran now has some 10,000 functioning centrifuges, and they have streamlined the enrichment process. Iran today has five tons of low-grade fissile material, enough, when converted to high-grade material, to make about five to six bombs; it also has about 175 pounds of medium-grade material, of which it would need about 500 pounds to make a bomb. It is believed that Iran's nuclear scientists estimate that it would take them nine months, from the moment they are given the order, to assemble their first explosive device and another six months to be able to reduce it to the dimensions of a payload for their Shahab-3 missiles, which are capable of reaching Israel.[15]

Israel has made it abundantly clear that it will take out Iran's nuclear capabilities. But there are all kinds of questions: What will happen when Israel strikes? How will they do it?

THE PATH TO PREEMPTION ·

There's no doubt that Israel is ready to hit Iran. Israel's top general, Chief of Staff Benny Gantz, said bluntly, "The military force is ready. Not only our forces, but other forces as well."[16] Of course, readiness is one thing, but execution is another. Most analysts maintain that an Israeli strike will "take the form of a complex air assault involving scores of planes that would have to penetrate Iranian air defenses and attack up to a couple of dozen targets simultaneously."[17] Due to the distance to Iran and the number of sites that must be hit, this operation will, by all accounts, be more sophisticated than anything ever attempted before.[18]

Experts believe Israel has three possible paths to Iran. First, there's a northern route along the Turkish-Syrian border that covers about 1300 miles. Second, the central route travels directly over Jordan and Iraq and cuts the distance to about 1000 miles. Third, the southern route flies over Saudi Arabia into Iran, and it is longer than the direct route. But sources claim that Saudi Arabia has already given Israel permission to fly its airspace for a strike against Iran. The path seems to be clear for an Israeli assault. The question is, Will Israel use planes (which would be a supreme logistical challenge), or could it decide to employ another method for hammering Iran's nuclear plants?

Some experts speculate that Israel may find it too challenging and risky to send aircraft and ground troops (or both) to take out the Iranian nuclear facilities. They believe Israel could simply launch nuclear missiles from submarines to incinerate the underground centrifuges.

> Israel has the ability to strike at Iran's nuclear facilities, many of them underground in hardened positions, using long-range F-15s armed with American supplied bunker buster bombs. But such an approach would be risky and might involve heavy casualties among Israeli pilots... A flotilla of nuclear armed submarines, positioned in the Persian Gulf perhaps, might provide an alternative way of taking out Iran's nuclear program...Israel might feel it is justified in launching a first strike against Iran with nuclear weapons. Nuclear weapons would be capable of penetrating the hardened, underground nuclear facilities in Iran and destroying them. They would also provide an object lesson, not just to Iran, but to any potential enemy of the Jewish state who contemplates a nuclear arsenal.[19]

Others agree Israel could opt for using submarines and even go nuclear in a devastating first strike. Israel is believed to have about 200 nuclear weapons:

> Aircraft are not the only means at Israel's disposal. It could also launch ballistic Jericho missiles with conventional warheads at Iran, according to a 2009 report by the Center for

Strategic and International Studies in Washington. Israel's three German-built Dolphin submarines are believed to be capable of carrying conventional and nuclear-tipped cruise missiles. They would have to transit through Egypt's Suez Canal—as one did in 2009—to reach the Gulf. Elite foot soldiers might be deployed to spot targets and possibly launch covert attacks. Far-flying drones could assist in surveillance and possibly drop bombs of their own.[20]

Israel announced in 2012 that it received its fourth German-made submarine capable of launching nuclear warheads. This Dolphin-class submarine, named *Tanin* ("alligator" in Hebrew), is considered one of the world's most advanced submarines. It expands Israel's fleet, which could be part of an attack against Iran. Israeli Defense Minister Ehud Barak noted that the new sub would increase Israel's capabilities and power "in the face of growing regional challenges."[21] Yoav Zitun writes in a similar article, "A fifth submarine is currently under construction and will arrive in Israel in 2014. Recently, the German government approved the sale of a sixth submarine, which is expected to arrive in Israel by 2017."[22]

Israel's submarines "can carry surface-to-surface Harpoon missiles capable of delivering a 227-kilogram warhead to a range of 130 kilometers and at high subsonic speed. Some suggest that the subs might be capable of carrying nuclear armed Popeye turbo cruise missiles, granting Israel clear second strike capabilities."[23]

Future Tense

Whenever and however the attack is launched, one thing is certain—a furious backlash will take place. Iran and its proxies will implement a counterstrike. But how extensive will it be? Could it trigger a regional war? Or even World War III? No one knows for sure, but it will certainly set off a series of events that will eventually lead to the fulfillment of biblical prophecy in the end times. But before we consider Iran's response, it's important to understand the mullah regime that controls Iran and the apocalyptic madness that drives it. This ideology will undoubtedly play an integral role in what will happen in the days ahead and on into the end times.

CHAPTER THREE

Show Me the Mahdi

An Apocalyptic, Genocidal Ideology Drives Iran

"Iran today is in the grip of yet a new wave of extremists. Its president, Mahmoud Ahmadinejad, is a revolutionary firebrand who has directly threatened the West. In his own words, 'We are in the process of an historical war between the World of Arrogance [i.e., the West] and the Islamic world.' His foreign policy ambition is an Islamic government for the whole world, under the leadership of the Mahdi, the absent imam of the Shiites—code language for the export of radical Islam. And he casts himself as Hitler reincarnated, calling for Israel to be 'wiped off the map.' Who can think that Iran poses no threat to world peace? History tells us that when madmen call for genocide, they usually mean it."[1]

Mortimer Zuckerman, *U.S. News and World Report*

In addition to Iran's hatred for Israel and its nuclear quest, as if those two factors weren't bad enough, Iran has an apocalyptic ideology, which is the belief that it can hasten the end of the world and bring about the global rule of Islam. Since the Islamic revolution in 1979 and the formation of the Islamic Republic of Iran, the Iranian mullah regime has led the nation in a deepening death spiral. Joel Rosenberg, an expert in Bible prophecy and geopolitics, graphically describes Iran's leadership as "an apocalyptic, genocidal death cult."[2] Those are strong words, but sadly, they are true. Iran's leadership is under the spell of a form of Shiite Islam known as "Twelver Shiism."

The majority of Muslims in the world today—about 85 percent—are Sunnis. Though Shiites are fewer in number overall, they are the dominant part of the population in Iran, Iraq and Bahrain. The difference between Shiites and Sunnis stems from a controversy over who is qualified to lead the religion. Understanding the particular strain of Shiite Islam that dominates Iran opens a frightening window into the thinking of its mullah regime and at least some of the motivation behind their actions.

HASTENING THE END

According to Shiite Islam, an imam is a spiritual leader who is allegedly a bloodline relative of the prophet Muhammad. There is a prophecy in Islam about the coming of the Twelfth Imam—Imam Muhammad Abul Qasim. It's believed by the Twelver sect that in AD 874, when the Twelfth Imam was five years old, he disappeared in the cave of the great mosque of Samarra without leaving any descendants. He was hidden by God. It's also taught that the Twelfth Imam was still active and communicated through messengers until AD 941. At that point they believe all communication and contact with this world was cut off. They call the Twelfth Imam the Hidden Imam and the *Mahdi* (Arabic for "rightly guided one"). Since the tenth century, they have been waiting for the Mahdi to emerge to lead them to victory and subjugate the world. According to Islamic teaching, he will return near the end of the world.

> The mullahs leading Iran's Islamic regime believe in the messianic return of the 12th and last Islamic messiah, Imam Mahdi. According to Shiite belief, Mahdi will reappear at the time of Armageddon, and his coming will be triggered by the destruction of Israel. In a recent statement, Grand Ayatollah Jafar Sobhani, a religious authority and a top Iranian "Twelver Shia"—one who believes in the 12th Imam—addressed the future world described in the Quran. "The Quran is the proof that the world will be controlled and managed by the forces of truth and that there will be one government ruling everyone throughout the world," he explained. The Quran promises—twice—the worldwide rule of Islam and its victory over all other religions, Sobhani said, and this

will only happen when the last descendant
of Muhammad, Imam Mahdi, returns and
takes the rule of Islam across the world. Ayatollah Khamenei referred to this prophecy in
a recent speech. "In light of the realization of
the divine promise by almighty God," he said,
"the Zionists and the Great Satan [America] will
soon be defeated. Allah's promise will be deliv-
ered, and Islam will be victorious."[3]

This end-time view, or eschatology, teaches that when
the Hidden Imam returns, he will rule the earth for seven
years, bringing about the Final Judgment and end of the
world. The mention of a seven-year rule for the Mahdi
is interesting to students of Bible prophecy because the
Bible predicts that the final Antichrist or false messiah
will hold sway over the earth for seven years, ruling the
entire world for the final half of the seven-year period.
Could the Islamic expectation of a messiah who will
rule for seven years set them up to initially accept such
a leader, one who will make a seven-year peace treaty
according to Daniel 9:27?

In any event, Iran's politics cannot be divorced from
its fundamental religious views about the Hidden Imam.
Iranian President Mahmoud Ahmadinejad believes in
the prophetic outline of the Twelfth Imam theology, and
he maintains that he is to do all he can to bring about its
fulfillment. He has reportedly said that he believes the
return of the Imam will occur in his lifetime, and he is in

his 50s. Many of his statements suggest that he believes
his reign is destined to bring about the end times. He has
a presidential obsession with what is known in Islam as
Mahdaviat. This is a technical religious term that means
"a belief in and efforts to prepare for the Mahdi."

As mayor of Tehran, Ahmadinejad persuaded the city
council to build a grand avenue in the city to prepare
for the coming of the Mahdi, the key figure in Islamic
eschatology. When he came to power as the president,
one of the initial acts of his government was to donate
$17 million to the Jamkaran Mosque, which is a popu-
lar pilgrimage site where Muslim devotees come to drop
messages in a well in which they believe the Hidden
Imam is hiding.

Ahmadinejad also believes the September 11 attacks
against the U.S. were a "big fabrication as a pretext for
the campaign against terrorism and a prelude for stag-
ing an invasion of Afghanistan."[4] Ironically, he denies
the Holocaust as a myth, yet wants to repeat it by wiping
Israel off the map. Infamous for his anti-Zionist
statements, Ahmadinejad said in April 2011, "A new
Middle East will emerge without the presence of the
United States and the Zionist regime [Israel], and their
allies in the near future."[5] He has threatened that "any-
body who recognizes Israel will burn in the fire of the
Islamic nation's fury."[6] At a celebration of "Army Day," he
blamed the U.S. for the unrest in the Middle East and for
working to create division between Shia and Sunni Muslims. He even said, "The era of Zionism and capitalism

has passed away." He also leveled threats against Saudi Arabia and other more moderate Gulf States.[7]

To demonstrate how deep the anti-Semitism runs among Iran's leadership, Iran's vice president used the lectern of an international antidrug conference in New York in June 2012 to deliver a baldly anti-Semitic speech, blaming Judaism's holy book for teaching how to suck blood from people. He also stated that Jews control the world drug trade and were responsible for the Bolshevik Revolution in Russia in 1917. [8]

Behind all the anti-Semitism and bravado lies the mystical Islamic theology that sees current events in the Middle East preparing the way for the coming of the Mahdi, Islam's messianic figure. Anton La Guardia makes this chilling observation about Ahmadinejad's "Apocalypse Now" theology:

> After a cataclysmic confrontation with evil and darkness, the Mahdi will lead the world to an era of universal peace...Indeed, the Hidden Imam is expected to return in the company of Jesus. Mr. Ahmadinejad appears to believe that these events are close at hand and that ordinary mortals can influence the divine timetable. The prospect of such a man obtaining nuclear weapons is worrying. The unspoken question is this: is Mr. Ahmadinejad now tempting a clash with the West because he feels safe in the belief of the imminent return of the Hidden Imam? Worse,

might he be trying to provoke chaos in the hope
of hastening his reappearance?[9]

Ahmadinejad firmly believes that the Mahdi controls
events in Iran and around the world, and he believes that
things are shaping up quickly for the Mahdi's coming.
For him, war with Israel and the U.S. and the ensuing
chaos is a kind of "welcome mat" for the Mahdi. In 2008,
he made this statement:

> The Imam Mahdi is in charge of the world and
> we see his hand directing all the affairs of the
> country. We must solve Iran's internal problems
> as quickly as possible. Time is lacking. A move-
> ment has started for us to occupy ourselves with
> our global responsibilities, which are arriving
> with great speed. Iran will be the focal point of
> the management of the world, thanks to God.
> In this region an event has to happen. The hand
> of God must appear and will make the roots of
> injustice in the world vanish.[10]

Ahmadinejad believes an end-time war will sweep
the Mahdi to power. Iran's participation in a regional or
even global conflict could be viewed as a self-fulfilling
prophecy.

FAST FACTS ABOUT THE MAHDI

- The Mahdi won't come in an odd year (Islamic calendar).
- He will appear in Mecca.
- He will travel from Mecca to Kufa (Iraq).
- He will be 40 years old at time of emergence.
- He will remove all injustice, bringing universal prosperity.
- Jesus will return with him and be his deputy.
- The Mahdi will wear a ring that belonged to King Solomon.
- He will carry the wooden staff of Moses.
- He will conquer his enemies, who will be led by the one-eyed Antichrist (Dajjal).
- He will rule for 7 years (some say 9 or 19 years).

ISLAMIC BELIEFS ABOUT THE MAHDI

- Islam's primary awaited Savior
- Descendant of Muhammad
- Caliph and Imam of Muslims worldwide
- Unparalleled political, military, and religious world leader

- Revealed after period of great turmoil and suffering on earth
- Establishes justice throughout the world
- Leads a revolution to establish a new world order
- Will go to war against all nations who oppose him
- Makes a seven-year peace treaty with a Jew of priestly lineage
- Conquers Israel for Islam and leads final battle against the Jews
- Rules for seven years centered in Jerusalem
- Causes Islam to be the only religion on earth
- Discovers biblical manuscripts that convince Jews to convert
- Brings the Ark of the Covenant from the Sea of Galilee to Jerusalem
- Has the power from Allah over wind, rain, and crops
- Will possess and distribute great wealth
- Face will shine like a star and will be loved by all

Joel Rosenberg summarizes the ideology that drives Iran:

> American leaders need to better understand Shia eschatology. The Twelfth Imam was a real, flesh-and-blood person who, like the eleven Shia leaders who went before him, was an Arab

male, a direct descendent of the founder of Islam, and was thought to have been divinely chosen to be the spiritual guide and ultimate human authority of the Muslim people. His actual name was Muhammad Ibn Hasan Ibn Ali, and it is generally believed by Shias that he was born in Samarra, Iraq, in AD 868. At a very young age, however, Ali vanished from society. Some say...the Mahdi's mother placed him in the well to prevent evil rulers from capturing him and killing him, and that little Ali subsequently became supernaturally invisible. This is where the term "Hidden Imam" is derived, as Shias believe that Ali is not dead but has simply been hidden from the sight of mankind—Shias refer to this as "occultation"—until the End of Days, when Allah will reveal him once again. Shias believe the Mahdi will return in the last days to establish righteousness, justice, and peace. When he comes, they say, the Mahdi will bring Jesus with him. Jesus will be a Muslim and will serve as his deputy, not as King of kings and Lord of lords as the Bible teaches, and he will force non-Muslims to choose between following the Mahdi or death. By most accounts, Shia scholars believe the Mahdi will first appear in Mecca and conquer the Middle East, then establish the headquarters of his global Islamic government—or caliphate—in Iraq. But there is not universal agreement. Some believe he will emerge from the well at the Jamkaran Mosque in Iran and then travel to Mecca and Iraq. Some say that he will conquer Jerusalem before establishing his caliphate in Iraq. Others believe Jerusalem must be conquered as a prerequisite to his return. None of this is actually written in the Kuran, and Sunnis reject this eschatology. But one thing that is fairly well agreed upon among devout "Twelvers" is that the Mahdi will end apostasy and purify corruption within Islam. He is expected to conquer the Arabian Peninsula, Jordan, Syria, "Palestine," Egypt and North Africa, and eventually the entire world. During this time, he and Jesus will kill between 60 and 80 percent of the world's population, specifically those who refuse to convert to Islam.[11]

WAITING FOR THE MAHDI

Iran is elated about the domino revolutions across the Middle East, except the one in its close ally, Syria. They view them as a sign of the Mahdi's coming and an open door to expand their influence.

Former U.S. ambassador to the U.N., John Bolton, has been a vigilant watchdog of Iran's regional and nuclear pursuits. He points out how Iran is seizing the opportunity created by the current Middle East to foster its own purposes:

> I think Iran is currently taking advantage of the turmoil in the Middle East to advance its own

hegemonic aspirations in the region. It's clearly interfered in the situation in Bahrain and it would like to interfere in Saudi Arabia. I think the real essence of the problem long-term is Iran's continuing support for terrorism, its continuing pursuit of nuclear weapons. As we focus on Libya or Egypt or other headlines of the day, we shouldn't lose sight that the great conflict, the great risk is an expansive Iran.[12]

Joel Rosenberg agrees:

The leaders in Tehran could not be more excited by the revolution now underway in Egypt and are praying the Mubarak regime collapses and the Muslim Brotherhood come to power. For them, such events would be dramatic new evidence that the End of Days has come, infidel Arab regimes are on the road to collapse, Western influence in the Mideast is declining, Israel is one step closer to being annihilated, and the Twelfth Imam is one step closer to arriving and establishing the worldwide Islamic kingdom known as the "caliphate."[13]

In 2011, a movie was released in Iran called *The Coming Is Near*. It is an eerie "second coming" propaganda video. It was distributed throughout the region to announce the soon arrival of the Mahdi and "instigate further uprisings in Arab countries."[14] Ryan Mauro describes its content:

> The Iranian government has produced a bone-chilling documentary that claims that Ayatollah Khamenei, President Ahmadinejad, and Hassan Nasrallah [the leader of Hezbollah] are talked about in Islamic prophecy as leaders who will wage war to bring about the arrival of the Hidden Imam, which the film says is "very close" to happening…The purpose of the film is to make the case that Iran is prophetically destined to lead the war against Islam's enemies, which is as a prelude to the appearance of the Hidden Imam, also called the Mahdi, who brings the final victory for Islam and reigns over the whole world. It uses current events to argue that "the final chapter has begun" and the Mahdi's arrival is imminent. Most disturbingly, it teaches that Khamenei, Ahmadinejad and Nasrallah are the individuals prophesied to make this happen.[15]

Here are some quotes and statements about the movie.[16]

- "Iran will soon usher in the end times."
- "The Iranian regime believes the chaos is divine proof that their ultimate victory is at hand."

- "It describes current events in the Middle East as a prelude to the arrival of the mythical twelfth Imam or Mahdi—the messiah figure who Islamic scriptures say will lead the armies of Islam to victory over all non-Muslims in the last days."

- "The video claims that Iran is destined to rise as a great power in the last days to help defeat America and Israel and usher in the return of the Mahdi. And it makes clear the Iranians believe that time is fast approaching."

- "The video claims that Iran is destined to rise as a great power in the last days to help defeat America and Israel and usher in the return of the Mahdi. And it makes clear the Iranians believe that time is fast approaching."

- "The video describes Ahmadinejad and Iran's Supreme Ayatollah Khamenei as the leaders who will bring about his return. It condemns the United States and Israel, and offers praise to the Muslim Brotherhood for helping to overthrow the government of Hosni Mubarak in Egypt."

Jonathon M. Seidl further describes the propaganda piece in this way:

The Hadith have clearly described the events and the various transformations of countries in the Middle East and also that of Iran in the age of the coming, said a narrator, who went on to say that America's invasion of Iraq was foretold by Islamic scripture—and that the Mahdi will one day soon rule the world from Iraq. The ongoing upheavals in other Middle Eastern countries like Yemen and Egypt—including the rise of the Muslim Brotherhood—are also analyzed as prophetic signs that the Mahdi is near—so is the current poor health of the king of Saudi Arabia, an Iranian rival…Iran's supreme leader, Ayatollah Khamenei, and Hassan Nasrallah, leader of Iran's terrorist proxy Hezbollah, are hailed as pivotal end times players, whose rise was predicted in Islamic scripture. The same goes for Iran's President Mahmoud Ahmadenijad, who the video says will conquer Jerusalem prior to the Mahdi's coming.[17]

Here's a chilling quote from the movie:

Therefore let us shout out loud that The Coming is soon and that evil should be fearful. We live with these thoughts every day and our lives are filled with The Coming of the last Imam. That human will reappear and fill the world with justice and establish his promised governance on earth. The very world has witnessed

too much bloodshed of the innocent for others
to build their palaces…It is in this very world
where the oppressors rule and this world that
Allah will command the last Imam to appear
and forever put an end to injustice. At that time,
the world will belong to the righteous.[18]

This is the Shiite Twelver view of the end times. It pre-
sents a vastly different view of the end of days than the
Bible. So this is the next logical question: Which one is
correct? Why should we believe what the Bible says any
more than the Quran? Is there any objective way to know
which of these competing eschatologies is true? Or if
either one carries the ring of truth? Why should anyone
believe the prophecies of the Bible as opposed to those in
the Quran or any other alleged holy book?

THE PROOF IS IN THE FULFILLMENT

Most people are probably not aware that more than
one-fourth of the Bible was prophetic at the time it was
written. The Bible is a book of prophecy. It contains
about 1000 prophecies, about 500 of which have already
been fulfilled down to the minutest detail. With this kind
of proven track record—500 prophecies fulfilled with
100 percent accuracy—we can believe with confidence
that the remaining 500 yet-to-be-fulfilled prophecies
will also come to pass at the appointed time. Someone
once commendably said, "We don't believe in prophecy

because it's contained in the Bible, but we believe in the Bible because it contains prophecy." Prophecy is the most credible proof of the uniqueness and divine inspiration of the Bible. Its importance can hardly be overstated. About 110 prophecies were fulfilled in the life and ministry of Jesus alone.

Fulfilled prophecy validates the Bible and all the precious truths it contains. Think about it. If hundreds of biblical prophecies have been meticulously, accurately fulfilled, then it stands to reason that what the Bible has to say about other things—such as the nature and character of God, creation, the nature of man, salvation, and the existence of heaven and hell—are 100 percent accurate as well. It also demonstrates that the Bible's content is not man-made but rather has its origins outside our own space-time continuum.[19]

The God of the Bible is so certain that only He can foretell the future that He issues a challenge to any would-be rivals to His place of supremacy in the universe. The basis of the challenge is that only the true God can accurately predict the future. Read what God says about His unique ability to forecast the future.

> "Present your case," the LORD says. "Bring forward your strong arguments," the King of Jacob says. Let them bring forth and declare to us what is going to take place; as for the former events, declare what they were, that we may consider them and know their outcome. Or announce

to us what is coming; declare the things that are
going to come afterward, that we may know that
you are gods; indeed, do good or evil, that we
may anxiously look about us and fear together.
Behold, you are of no account, and your work
amounts to nothing; he who chooses you is an
abomination (Isaiah 41:21-24).

Islam makes no real claim that the Quran has foretold events that have come to pass. It lays out an elabo-
rate end-time scenario, but provides no objective basis for
believing that it will come to fruition. One must take it
solely on faith. The Bible, on the other hand, gives overwhelming, credible evidence that its prophecies come
true and therefore provides a solid basis for our confidence that its prognostications about the future will
also come to pass. The Bible has a proven track record
we can put to the test. This means that the prophecies
of the Bible, even including the ones about Iran in Ezekiel 38–39, will be fulfilled just as the Bible says. We can
count on it. This means that in a strange ironic twist the
idea that Iran's leaders can speed up the coming of the
end times might actually be true, but it will not be the
scenario they have envisioned.

What Will They Do?

Iran's apocalyptic beliefs and the notion that they can
hasten the events of the end of days, heightens the fear of
Israel that Iran could get its hands on nuclear weapons.

Someone with these beliefs can never be allowed to possess the bomb. They cannot be counted on to act rationally and with the normal sense of self-preservation.

All of this raises a critical question: What will Iran do? Do the mullahs really believe the final chapter has begun and that they can help bring it to fruition? Will their apocalyptic ideology drive them to seize the opportunity to unleash a regional or even global conflict that will bring the Mahdi, or do they have the survival instinct that will lead them to hold their cards until some later time? Time will tell. But ultimately, according to the ancient prophecies of Ezekiel, Iran will join with a coalition of allies to attack Israel at the end of days. We may be witnessing the beginning of the buildup for this end-time war.

CHAPTER FOUR

Unleashing the Dogs of Terror

Hamas and Hezbollah Strike Israel

"I think we need to be prepared for all options. It is most likely that Hezbollah will join in and will strike Israel. Then Syria could be part of it, Gaza could be part of it. We need to be prepared for a multi-front conflict if we go to Iran. A multi-front conflict could affect all of Israel. Hezbollah is prepared to shower about 1,000 missiles and rockets on Israel per day of fighting, among them, about 100 missiles on Tel Aviv, so this city (would be) completely different than it is today. And this is something we haven't experienced in the 64 years of Israel's independence.... So these will be tough times for the Israeli public. It's going to be a challenge."[1]

Alon Ben-David, Israeli military correspondent

"The fallout of a preemptive strike would be painful.... But we need to think of the tradeoff: A nuclear bomb could be devastating for the State of Israel."[2]

Ehud Barak, Israeli Defense Minister

In May 2012, the vice president of Iran, Mohammad Reza Rahimi, visited the stronghold of the terrorist group Hezbollah in Lebanon and met with the Hezbollah Secretary-General Sayyed Hasan Nasrallah. The leader of Hezbollah reiterated his support for Iran and hatred for Israel. At one point during the visit, they traveled to the Lebanon–Israel border and stood "in front of a board that carried a famous statement by Iran's late supreme leader Ayatollah Khomeini—'Israel must be eliminated'—and amid an array of pictures of Khomeini, Khamenei and Ahmadinejad. The Iranian Vice President said he was proud and happy to be in 'this blessed spot.'"[3] This chilling scene says all that needs to be said about the posture of Iran and Hezbollah toward Israel.

According to one estimate, there are currently 200,000 missiles aimed at the nation of Israel.[4] Iran alone has hundreds of Shahab missiles armed with warheads that can reach Israel. When Israel hits Iran, what will the response be?

Some believe Israel will be bombarded by a barrage of rockets and missiles unlike anything it has ever experienced. Others surmise that the response will be measured. No one knows for sure, but some reaction will certainly come. How extensive will the counterstrike be? How many of the available missiles will be launched into Israel? Who will participate—Iran, Hamas, Hezbollah, Palestinian Islamic Jihad, possibly even Syria and Egypt? Maybe Russia? How will Israel respond to the counterstrikes? What will their second strike look like? These are the nagging questions that keep world leaders awake at night.

What Will Iran Do?

Opinions regarding what Iran will do are all over the place. There has been no shortage of threatening, dismissive rhetoric out of Iran. Brigadier General Mostafa Izadi, deputy chief of staff of Iran's armed forces, had this to say:

> They cannot do the slightest harm to the (Iranian) revolution and the system. If the Zionist regime takes any (military) actions against Iran, it would result in the end of its labors. If they act logically, such threats amount to a psychological war but if they want to act illogically, it is they who will be destroyed.[5]

Some experts maintain that Iran, despite its public bravado and intimidating language, will make a measured response toward Israel, possibly launching "a handful of rockets at Tel Aviv as an angry gesture," or maybe even doing nothing at all directly.[6]

The New York Times offers an optimistic view:

> Many experts have predicted that Iran would try to carefully manage the escalation after an Israeli first strike in order to avoid giving the United States a rationale for attacking with its far superior forces. Thus, it might use proxies to set off car bombs in world capitals or funnel high explosives to insurgents in Afghanistan to attack American and NATO troops.[7]

This optimism, however, might be misplaced.

Under the opposite scenario, Iran could choose to fire hundreds of missiles into Israel, even into the heart of Tel Aviv, Israel's most populated city. It could even hit U.S. interests in the Gulf region and could release its proxies to inflict terror and misery against Israel. All-out war would result. This is the nightmare outcome.

THE SURROGATES STRIKE

The uncertainty about Iran's direct response is multiplied when considering what its surrogate states will do. Hezbollah has made bold threats, and Hamas continually fires rockets into southern Israel. The question is, how far will they go to retaliate on Iran's behalf?

HORROR FROM HEZBOLLAH

Hezbollah, which means "Party of God," was founded in the early 1980s by a Lebanese follower of Ayatollah Khomeini and members of Iran's Islamic Revolutionary Guards Corps in Lebanon. It is a proxy or surrogate for Iran. Hezbollah does Iran's bidding.

Prior to September 11, Hezbollah was supported by Syria and Iran and was responsible for the deaths of more Americans than any other terrorist group. Hezbollah orchestrated and carried out simultaneous homicide bombings of U.S. Marine barracks and French paratrooper headquarters in Beirut on April 18, 1983. The attack killed 241 Marines, the highest loss of life among

U.S. soldiers since the Vietnam War. As a result of the attack, America withdrew from Lebanon. Iran not only founded Hezbollah, it funds and arms them as well. Israel fought a bloody month-long war against Hezbollah in the summer of 2006. Hezbollah and Iran loudly proclaimed victory in the war, and Hezbollah has hardened its launching sites and expanded its arsenal in the days following 2006. Hezbollah is a formidable foe.

In May 2012, the head of Hezbollah in Lebanon, Sayyed Hassan Nasrallah, threatened Israel in light of any Israeli attack against Iran.

> Today we are not only able to hit Tel Aviv as a city but, God willing, we are able to hit specific targets in Tel Aviv and anywhere in occupied Palestine...For every building destroyed in Dahiya [Hezbollah's stronghold in a suburb of southern Beirut] a building will be destroyed in Tel Aviv...The days when we were forced from our homes and they were not forced from theirs are over...The days when we were afraid and they were not are over...And we say to them: The time has come when we will remain and you will be the ones who disappear.[8]

In a chilling article titled, "Hezbollah Iran Missiles Slam Hadera Israel—Nuclear War Approaching?," Joel Leyden writes the following:

The only good thing about the terror group Hezbollah (Hizbollah) or Islam Party of God is that they keep their promises. Just two days ago Hezbollah terror leader Hassan Nasrallah said from Lebanon that he would strike Tel Aviv, Israel with missiles if the Israel Defense Forces attacked parts of central Beirut.

A few hours ago, Hezbollah launched three Iran missiles at the Israel city of Hadera. Hadera is 70 miles south from the Lebanese border and 30 miles north from Tel Aviv. The strike was the deepest inside Israel to date in the fighting between the Jewish state and the Lebanon-based terrorists. Hezbollah is believed to have missiles that can reach Tel Aviv, but such an attack would trigger a massive Israel response. One that would most likely include Syria and Iran. Iran admitted today that it did indeed supply long-range Zelzal-2 missiles to Hizbullah. The longer-range Zelzal missiles, manufactured by Iran…are capable of reaching Tel Aviv, Jerusalem and Beer Sheva in the Negev. In making this announcement, Iran reinforced its statement of "wiping Israel off the map" and though bullets are not flying yet between Israel and Iran, both nations are very much at war.[9]

Another angle to the Iranian retaliation strategy is that Israeli intelligence believes Iran and Hezbollah have planted about 40 terrorist sleeper cells across the globe,

ready to hit Israeli and Jewish targets if Iran decides to
seek revenge.[10]

In October 2012, Israel shot down an Iranian-made
drone flying over Israel that had come from Hezbollah in
Lebanon. Drone attacks could be part of any retaliation
by Hezbollah.

Any attack by Israel against Hezbollah in Lebanon
could also possibly draw Syria into the fray leading to
all-out war. Hezbollah is supported by Syria, which is
reeling under the duress of civil war, but the prospect of
fighting a common foe could be what the beleaguered
government needs to divert attention from the internal disintegration of the country. With the rise of the
Muslim Brotherhood in Egypt, who have been loudly
applauded by Iran, the Egyptians could also seize the
opportunity to strike their nemesis or at least abrogate
the peace agreement they have with Israel. We already
know that most Egyptians want to annul the Camp
David Accords. (The peace treaty known as the Camp
David Accords was signed by the Egyptian president
Anwar Sadat and the Israeli prime minister Menachem
Begin in 1979.) This could be their opportunity to wipe
out the peace agreement with Israel.

Help from Hamas?

Hamas was founded in 1987 in Gaza by Sheikh
Ahmad Yassin. Hamas was created shortly before the
December 1987 Intifada (uprising) as an aggressive

militant, Palestinian offshoot of the Muslim Brotherhood, which is a religious, political, and social movement
founded in Egypt that is dedicated to the gradual victory of Islam. "Hamas" is an Arabic acronym for Islamic
Resistance Movement, and it means "zeal."[11] Since its
inception, Hamas has been committed to destroying the
Jewish state and replacing it with an Islamic state in all of
Israel.

One of the most surprising events for Israel in the last
decade was the success of the terrorist group Hamas in
the Palestinian elections in 2006. Hamas scored a stunning upset in the January 25, 2006, parliamentary elections, routing Fatah, and winning 74 seats in the 132-seat
legislature.[12] Hamas now rules the Gaza area to the south
and west of Israel.

Concerning the response of Hamas to an Israeli preemptive strike against Iran, Enad Benari provides this
insight:

> Iran hopes that Hamas and Islamic Jihad, both
> of which are centered in the Gaza Strip to the
> south and west of Israel, will light up the south-
> ern front as Hezbollah does the same thing in
> the north. Hamas' Gaza Prime Minister Ismail
> Haniyeh reiterated...that his organization will
> not be dragged into war against Israel if the Jew-
> ish State decides to attack Iran's nuclear facilities.
> "Hamas is an organization which works in the
> Palestinian arena and operates in a way that is
> compatible with the interests of the Palestinians,"

Haniyeh said in an interview, according to Israel's Channel 10 News. Haniyeh stressed that the Islamic Republic did not seek any support from Hamas should Israel decide to attack Iran. "Iran did not ask for anything and we think it does not need us," said Haniyeh, adding that an Israeli attack in Iran would lead to serious consequences in the Middle East. "I cannot predict what will happen, but such a battle would have implications on the region." Several months ago, senior Hamas official Salah Bardawil claimed the terror group will not do Iran's bidding in any war with Israel. "If there is a war between two powers, Hamas will not be part of such a war," Bardawil said, adding, "Hamas is not part of military alliances in the region. Our strategy is to defend our rights."[13]

Of course, it could be that Hamas is bluffing and trying to lure Israel into a false sense of security if it hits Iran. However, as Israel's closest and most vulnerable neighbor, Hamas may believe that staying on the sidelines is in its own best interest. Time will tell.

STRIKE TWO

If Israel launches a preemptive strike against Iran's nuclear facilities, it will essentially be "all in" at that point. All its chips will be in the center of the table. Israel believes it can successfully weather the retaliation that will come from Iran. Ehud Barak says, "A war is no picnic," but he believes any response would be bearable. He said, "There will not be 100,000 dead or 10,000 dead or 1,000 dead. The state of Israel will not be destroyed."[14]

Israel has pledged that any counterstrike against Israel by Iran's proxies, Hezbollah and Hamas, or even by Iran itself will be met with overwhelming force. This is where the whole situation becomes very dicey and could begin to spin out of control and bring other nations into the mix. The warnings from Israel about its second strike capability are strong and unwavering.

> A senior Israeli military officer warned that any Hizbullah retaliation to an attack on Iran's nuclear facilities would prompt Israel to launch a war in Lebanon. The officer, who spoke to the *British Telegraph* on Sunday, said the war would be so ferocious that it would take a decade to rebuild the villages it destroys. The warning comes after months of heightened speculation that the Israeli government is considering unilateral military action against Iran's nuclear installations. The officer urged the Lebanese people not to be drawn into a war for which they, rather than Iran, would bear the brunt of Israel's anger. "The situation in Lebanon after this war will be horrible," the officer told the Telegraph. "They will have to think about whether they want it or not. I hope that Iran will not push them into a war that Iran will not pay the price for but that Lebanon will."[15]

A senior Israeli official said, "Despite the inevitable international outcry, Israel would be left with no choice but to lay waste to swathes of southern Lebanon because Hizbollah has entrenched itself so deeply within the civilian population."[16] This is serious stuff. It sounds like Israel is prepared to hammer Hezbollah into the dust.

DEFENDING THE HOME FRONT

Israel is preparing to defend itself against the expected barrage of rockets from Hezbollah and Hamas and missiles from Iran that will probably come when Israel launches a preemptive strike. Israel is on the cutting edge of new technology that could lead to greater security and protection. While there have been recent chinks in the armor, Israel still has the most powerful military in the region and is always working to come up with better ways for defending itself.

The Israel Defense Forces have deployed a new cutting-edge anti-rocket system called the "Iron Dome." The surface- to-air missile system is designed to combat the rise in rocket fire against Israel. The United States originally provided $200 million for the project, but it has approved an additional $680 million. The U.S. provides $3 billion in security assistance annually to the Jewish state. An upgraded system called Iron Dome 2.0 is in the works. So what is the Iron Dome?

> Iron Dome is a $200 million investment consisting of cameras, radar, launchers, and a control

system. It tracks incoming rockets and is designed to strike down rockets within seconds of being launched. Previously, rockets have gone undetected by Israel's high-tech weaponry. Their short flight path, which takes only a few seconds, has made them difficult to track...The system is capable of detecting whether or not a rocket should be shot down. If a rocket is aimed for a remote area and is unlikely to result in casualties, the system will allow the rocket to land.[17]

Yaakov Katz reports some additional details of the Iron Dome in the *Jerusalem Post*:

As of May [2012], Israel possesses four Iron Dome batteries in operation and the air force plans to deploy an additional three over the coming year...The $680 million in [U.S.] aid will enable Israel to purchase three to four more batteries and accompanying interceptors. Since its deployment last year, Iron Dome batteries have intercepted nearly 100 Katyusha and Kassam rockets fired into Israel from the Gaza Strip. In addition to funding for new batteries, Congress also supports the development of Arrow 3—Israel's futuristic defense system against ballistic missiles—as well as David's Sling, the medium-range missile defense system under development by Raytheon and Rafael Advanced Defense Systems. Iron Dome is designed to defend against rockets at a range of 4 to 70 km. Each battery consists of a mini multi-mission radar manufactured by Israel Aerospace Industries and three launchers, each equipped with 20 interceptors called Tamirs. The radar enables Iron Dome operators to predict the impact site of the enemy rocket. If the rocket is slated to hit an open area, the operator may decide not to intercept. Each interceptor costs between $50,000-$100,000 and usually two are fired at rockets slated for interception.[18]

Obviously, Iron Dome is not foolproof and can't protect every location in Israel, but it does further reveal the kind of military success Israel has enjoyed. The Iron Dome has brought down 80 percent of rockets fired into southern Israel from the Gaza Strip.[19] It gives Israel a sense of security, albeit tenuous, and will soften the blow of any Hamas-Hezbollah onslaught.

In addition to the Iron Dome rocket shield, Israel has a missile defense system called "Magic Wand" or "David's Sling" that defends against medium-range missiles. A third air defense system, which protects against ballistic missiles, is called Arrow 2 with an upgraded version in the works called Arrow 3.

Arrow consists of three main components: a phased array radar, a fire control center, and a high-altitude interceptor missile. The phased array radar, known as "Green Pine," is capable of detecting incoming warheads at a distance of 500 kilometers. This provides adequate radar coverage, since missiles launched at Israel from other Middle Eastern nations will not appear over the horizon before this distance. The system is designed to work quickly and efficiently. As soon as Green Pine detects an incoming missile, the fire control center, called "Citron Tree," launches its interceptor missile. The 23-foot long interceptor shoots toward the threat at nine times the speed of sound, and reaches a height of 30 miles in less than three minutes. Once it gets within two seconds of its target, Arrow's optical detectors aims for the incoming missile's warhead. The interceptor's own explosive warhead detonates within 40 to 50 yards of the missile, allowing Arrow to miss its target and still neutralize the threat.[20]

Israel has done everything within its power to prepare for war and self-defense, and all of these preparations may be put to the test sooner rather than later. Yet no matter how prepared they may be, when the fog of war sets in as a result of a preemptive strike, protecting their tiny land against the backlash could prove to be the most daunting challenge they've faced in their modern history.

AMERICAN ASSISTANCE OR ABSENCE?

The great X-factor in Israel's attack on Iran and its aftermath is the United States. What will America do? Will we come to Israel's aid or choose to sit this one out?

No one knows for sure. There are so many variables in play that no one can say for sure. Israel may not even give the U.S. advanced notice of its strike. But one thing is certain—the U.S. will play some role in the conflict if things begin to spiral out of control. This raises an often asked and often debated issue: What is America's role in the end times? Does the Bible provide any clues about the future of America?

CHAPTER FIVE

What Will Happen to America?

Bible Prophecy Is Silent About America's Role in the End Times

> *"America is not mentioned anywhere in the Bible, implying that it would be crippled or taken out of the picture in some way."* [1]
>
> **Glenn Beck** (April 2009)

People everywhere are wondering where the Middle East crisis is headed. All eyes are on Israel and Iran. This book is primarily about these two nations and how current events involving them point toward biblical prophecy.

But the number one question today in Bible prophecy is, where is America in the end times? America is the key player in the world today and figures heavily in the ongoing events in the Middle East. America is the lone superpower in the world. Will this continue into the end times? What is America's role in all this?

One thing is certain: Americans are war-weary as the conflict in Iraq has ended and the over one decade-long war in Afghanistan grinds to an uncertain end. We all wonder if America will be dragged into another Middle East conflict. Will America lead the attack against Iran's nukes, will it aid Israel in some way, or will it remain on the sidelines? Will Iran target U.S. interests if Israel strikes? What does the Bible say, if anything, about America's future? I've been asked this last question so many times that I wrote a book to address all the issues related to America in Bible prophecy. The book is titled *The Late Great United States: What Bible Prophecy Reveals about America's Last Days*. The thesis of the book is that America is not mentioned in the Bible, either directly or indirectly and that this silence is significant. America is not "Babylon the great" (Revelation 17–18), the unnamed nation (Isaiah 18), the ten lost tribes of Israel, or the "young lions" of Tarshish (Ezekiel 38:13 KJV). America is missing in action in the end-time prophecies of the Bible.

The Scriptures reveal that the major superpower in the end times, at least by the midpoint of the Tribulation, will be a reunited Roman Empire (Revelation 13:4). This dominance by the nations in a revived Roman Empire can only be explained in light of America's decline. Prophecy scholar John Walvoord sees no major end-time role for America:

Although conclusions concerning the role of America in prophecy in the end time are necessarily tentative, the Scriptural evidence is sufficient to conclude that America in that day will not be a major power and apparently does not figure largely in either the political, economic, or religious aspects of the world.[2]

Charles Ryrie agrees:

The Bible has made crystal clear the destiny of many nations. Babylon, Persia, Greece, Rome, Egypt, Russia, and Israel...But not so with the United States...The Bible's silence concerning the future of the United States might well mean that she will play no prominent role in the end time drama. A nation does not have to be named in order to be identified in Bible prophecy. When Ezekiel described the future Russian invasion he used the phrase "remote parts of the north" (38:15). Surely some prophet would have predicted something about those countries or peoples in the remote parts of the West if God had intended a major end-time role for them in the Western Hemisphere. The fact is that no one did.... Instead, we are led to conclude that the United States will be neutralized, subordinated, or wiped out, thus having little or no part in the political and military affairs of the end time.[3]

To be sure, I don't want to see the United States decline. I love this country, but it seems unlikely to me that the United States will play a key role in the end times. But what could reduce America to a subordinate role? What kind of event could bring America to its knees? While we cannot speak with certainty at this point—since the Bible doesn't tell us—we can make some educated guesses. Several plausible scenarios fit the current world situation. They could occur alone…or in a fatal combination. In the last few years, we have witnessed major developments on three fronts that threaten the continued role of America as the world's superpower. These three fronts are moral (internal decay), military (external threat of nuclear terror), and monetary (economic hazard of a diminishing role for America and the dollar). Let's briefly consider each of these mounting perils.

Moral Meltdown

The news on the moral front for America is not good. We are rapidly approaching a disastrous 50-percent out-of-wedlock birthrate. The dreaded scourge of abortion continues unabated with the total now over 50 million since 1973. Pornography is an industry of more than $12 billion, and it is infecting our young people every day. According to the Centers for Disease Control, 26 percent of American girls between the ages of 14 and 19 have at least one sexually transmitted disease.[4] Added to all this, the homosexual movement continues to propel its agenda forward, tragically affirming America's deepening slide into the death spiral of judgment described in Romans 1:26-32. This passage describes how God's wrath is revealed against nations in giving people over or abandoning them to the ravaging consequences of their sin.

> God gave them over to dishonorable passions. For their women exchanged the natural sexual relations for unnatural ones, and likewise the men also abandoned natural relations with women and were inflamed in their passions for one another. Men committed shameless acts with men and received in themselves the due penalty for their error. And just as they did not see fit to acknowledge God, God gave them over to a depraved mind, to do what should not be done. They are filled with every kind of unrighteousness, wickedness, covetousness, malice. They are rife with envy, murder, strife, deceit, hostility. They are gossips, slanderers, haters of God, insolent, arrogant, boastful, contrivers of all sorts of evil, disobedient to parents, senseless, covenant-breakers, heartless, ruthless. Although they fully know God's righteous decree that those who practice such things deserve to die, they not only do them but also approve of those who practice them (NET).

As you read these verses, did you catch the three-fold repetition of that phrase "God gave them over" (verses

24,26,28)? This describes how God judges people by abandoning them to their sin and how this sin is expressed first in sexual revolution and then in homosexual revolution. It all started in the 1960s, and since then, that is the tragic trajectory America has taken. Homosexual marriage is now permitted in Iowa, Massachusetts, Vermont, New Hampshire, Connecticut, New York, and the District of Columbia. Several other states offer civil unions or domestic partnerships. More states are considering similar legislation as the dominos continue to fall. A *Washington Post*/ABC survey in March 2011 found 53 percent of Americans now support gay marriage. An Associated Press poll in August 2010 found 52 percent of Americans think the federal government should extend legal recognition to married gay couples, up from 46 percent the year before.[5] The sexual revolution of Romans 1:24-25 has been followed with shocking suddenness by the homosexual revolution of Romans 1:26-27.

Americans have a growing sense that things are not right—that we are coming off the rails morally. In a recent Gallup poll (May 2010), Americans were asked about their perception of moral values in the country: "How would you rate the overall state of moral values in this country—as excellent, good, only fair, or poor?"

This is how they responded:

- 45 percent said poor.

- 15 percent said excellent or good.

They were also asked about where they thought our moral values are headed: "Right now, do you think the state of moral values in the country as a whole is getting better or worse?"

- 76 percent said it was getting worse.

- 14 percent said it was getting better.

Some Americans were asked to give more details about what they perceive as moral values:

> Most commonly, respondents see a lack of respect for other people and a more general decline in moral values and standards. But the responses are quite varied. Specifically, some blame the perceived decline on poor parenting—specifically, parents not instilling proper values in their children. Some cite the poor examples of U.S. leaders in government and business who find themselves embroiled in ethical or moral scandals. And some reference larger societal factors, such as rising crime and violence, Americans turning away from God, church and religion, and the breakdown of the typical two-parent family.[6]

It is clear that America is hemorrhaging from within. Thomas Macauley, a British Parliamentarian, wrote these sobering words about the United States in 1857. "Your Republic will be as fearfully plundered and laid waste by barbarians in the 20th century as the Roman Empire was in the 5th century, with this difference—the Huns and Vandals who ravaged the Roman Empire came from without, and your Huns and Vandals will have been engendered within your own country." It now appears that the Huns and Vandals of moral rot are upon us. When open sexual sin is condoned followed by a homosexual revolution, Romans 1 says that judgment has already begun. When people ask, "When is God going to judge America?" the answer is clear: He already is. He is judging America by abandoning her, by giving her over to her own wicked desires. How much longer until the final collapse? No one knows. But we need to be praying for our nation and doing all we can to live godly lives and promote righteousness.

Military Attack

Due to its geographic position and military might, America has enjoyed a level of peace and security most other nations envy. The U.S. never faced the serious danger of an attack on its own soil until December 7, 1941, and then on September 11, 2001, by Islamic terrorists. While any further terrorist attacks on American soil would be tragic, the most serious external threat America faces is the nightmarish threat of nuclear terror—a nuclear 9/11. The threat may seem far-fetched to many, but there are people who wake up every morning and think and live every day with the chief purpose of their lives to bring havoc and ultimately nuclear devastation to America. Experts warn the threat is growing and may be more likely than not in the next decade.

Pakistan is growing more unstable all the time and has an impressive nuclear arsenal that is expected to reach 200 nukes by 2021. North Korea could weaponize its program. Iran is trying to reach the nuclear finish line and develop a deliverable nuclear weapon. A nuclear device provided by Iran could be detonated in the United States by terrorists. While no one wants to even think about it, America would be the prime target, along with Israel, for any nuclear terrorist efforts. The horrifying threat of a nuclear 9/11 is growing. Our leaders know this and are doing all they can to stem the tide, but intelligence and military might can only do so much. It's only a matter of time until terrorists are able to get their hands on nuclear material and can detonate either a dirty bomb (which spreads harmful radiation in a city) or an actual nuclear device. Of course, either of these scenarios would cause untold loss in human life and economic catastrophe, not to mention the lingering psychological effects that may leave the nation in a state from which it will be unable to recover.

MONEY MATTERS

The effects of the economic tsunami that hit the world in 2008 are still being felt. Everyone knows that the American economy is still fragile and will fail if serious changes are not implemented soon. Unemployment still hovers above eight percent. Entitlement spending will doom America if changes are not made. It's no great surprise why America's stock is dropping. At the time of this writing, America's national debt stands at a staggering $16.3 trillion dollars…and counting. The numbers on America's infamous debt clock near New York's Times Square have been spinning like a high-speed fan. More and more Americans are looking to the government for support. Cradle to grave entitlements have led to what is being dubbed a "nanny state." The words of Thomas Jefferson are a stark reminder and warning: "A government big enough to give you everything you want is strong enough to take everything you have." According to the Bible, that's exactly where this all is ultimately headed under the Antichrist.

Time magazine ran an article on April 6, 2009, titled "Is the Almighty Dollar Doomed?" It chronicles the growing consensus that the days of the dollar reserve system are numbered.[7]

Rich Miller and Simon Kennedy point out in their online article just how much the U.S. is declining on the economic front:

> "It's the passing of an era," said Robert Hormats, vice chairman of Goldman Sachs International, who helped prepare summits for presidents Gerald R. Ford, Jimmy Carter and Ronald Reagan. "The U.S. is becoming less dominant while other nations are gaining influence."[8]

According to the Office of Management and Budget, entitlement spending—Medicare, Medicaid, Social Security, and other benefit programs—now accounts for 60 percent of all spending. According to *USA Today*, "The real drivers of looming deficits are Medicare, projected to grow from $516 billion this year to $932 billion in 2018, and Social Security, forecast to grow from $581 billion this year to $966 in 2018 as Baby Boomers retire."[9]

The United States could collapse under the weight of its own excess, greed, and massive government mind-set.

Debt is not just an economic issue. It bleeds over into other key areas as well. It threatens the security (even the continued existence) of nations. For instance, the U.S. Air Force says it needs more money to maintain the U.S. dominance of the skies that it's enjoyed for decades. The American military machine is aging due to the wars in Iraq and Afghanistan, and new fighters and new technology carry a bigger and bigger price tag. If the U.S. economy hits hard enough times, money allocations will have to be prioritized, and hard decisions will have to be made. More of the limited funds going to entitlements and other government programs will mean less to defense and could leave the United States more vulnerable than ever in modern times. Past empires have fallen under the crushing weight of massive debt service and their resulting inability to fund their military. Hapsburg Spain, prerevolutionary France, the Ottoman Empire, and even the British in the buildup to World War II all went the same way.[10]

Newsweek ran a cover article on December 7, 2009, with the title "How Great Empires Fall: Steep Debt, Slow Growth and High Spending Kill Empires—And America Could Be Next." The cover had a gripping picture of the U.S. Capitol building upside down. The feature article in *Newsweek* was titled "An Empire at Risk." Here are few key excerpts from this insightful article by Niall Ferguson.

> We won the Cold War and weathered 9/11 but now economic weakness is endangering our global power...if the United States succumbs to a fiscal crisis, as an increasing number of economic experts fear it may, then the entire balance of global economic power could shift...If the United States doesn't come up soon with a credible plan to restore the federal budget to balance over the next 5 to 10 years, the danger is very real that a debt crisis could lead to a major weakening of American power.[11]

Ferguson notes the critical nexus between a nation's debt explosion and the inevitable weakening of its military arsenal. "This is how empires begin to decline. It begins with a debt explosion. It ends with an inexorable reduction in the Army, Navy, and Air Force...As interest payments eat into the budget, something has to give—and that something is nearly always defense expenditure. On the Pentagon's present plan, defense spending is set to fall from above 4 percent now to 3.2 percent of GDP in

2015 and to 2.6 percent of GDP by 2028."[12] It's known as the "arithmetic of imperial decline."[13] Without radical fiscal reform, America, unable to expend the necessary resources for its own defense, could become the next great superpower to fall irreparably on the imperial ashheap of history.

America's financial woes could also eventually lead to a much more isolationist stance. While in today's global society it's impossible not to interact economically and politically with other nations, Americans are weary of being the world's police force. With one major war just ended and another one grinding ever so slowly to a halt, and crushing debt problems, it is not difficult to envision America pulling back on the international front. If this happens, it could pave the way for the reunited Roman Empire and other nations to assume greater leadership roles, further paving the way for Antichrist's arrival.

THE RAPTURE AND THE END OF AMERICA AS WE KNOW IT

While the three scenarios we just discussed—moral decay, military threat, or monetary collapse—could happen alone or in a crippling combination, there's one other event that could suddenly end life in America as we know it. That event is the rapture.

When the rapture occurs, every living believer in Jesus Christ on earth will be whisked to heaven in a moment. In the time it takes to blink your eye every living believer in Jesus Christ will disappear from this earth, and the bodies of God's people who have died will be raised and rejoined with their perfected spirits. The rapture is vividly described in two key New Testament passages.

> Now I say this, brethren, that flesh and blood cannot inherit the kingdom of God; nor does the perishable inherit the imperishable. Behold, I tell you a mystery; we will not all sleep, but we will all be changed, in a moment, in the twinkling of an eye, at the last trumpet; for the trumpet will sound, and the dead will be raised imperishable, and we will all be changed. For this perishable must put on the imperishable, and this mortal must put on immortality (1 Corinthians 15:50-53).
>
> For the Lord Himself will descend from heaven with a shout, with the voice of the archangel and with the trumpet of God, and the dead in Christ will rise first. Then we who are alive and remain will be caught up together with them in the clouds to meet the Lord in the air, and so we shall always be with the Lord. Therefore comfort one another with these words (1 Thessalonians 4:16-17).

Add in the rapture to all the other surging problems, and America will become a second-rate nation in the twinkling of an eye. The rapture will change everything! While every nation has believers, America has a larger percentage of believers than any other nation on earth. Think about the Dow Jones the next day. The unpaid mortgages. The loss of tax revenue. The cascade of bank failures. The immediate, sudden extraction of all the salt and light from the U.S. may be God's final judgment on America.

The rapture will be the trigger that sets the other events of the end times in motion. After the rapture, there will be a time of further preparation as events quickly begin to line up for the commencement of the end times. Out of the chaos that ensues from the rapture, a group of ten leaders will emerge from a revived form of the Roman Empire. Eventually, a strong man will emerge and begin to rise to power. The event that will catapult him to world power will be the signing of a peace agreement with Israel (more about this in the next chapter). The execution of this treaty will begin the clicking of the end-time clock as the world enters the time known as the Tribulation.

WHAT CAN WE DO?

No one on earth knows when the rapture will occur and America will fall. In the meantime, we must never forget to follow God's domestic policy for our nation by praying earnestly for our nation and leaders (1 Timothy 2:1-2) and living righteous lives (Proverbs 14:34), and to fulfill God's foreign policy by sharing the good news with the nations (Romans 10:15) and blessing the Jewish people (Genesis 12:1-3). We must remember that the fate of a nation is not ultimately dependent upon politics, military might, or economics, but on righteousness, goodness, and mercy.

In recent years America has placed itself on slippery ground by undermining its support for Israel. While America is not obligated to agree with every policy decision Israel makes, the Scripture is clear that nations are cursed or blessed by God based on their treatment of the Jewish people. History has borne this out. I like to say that every time someone has tried to wipe out the Jewish people, the Jews end up with a holiday. With Pharaoh they got Passover, with Haman in the book of Esther they got Purim, with Antiochus Epiphanes they got Hanukkah, and with Hitler they got May 14, 1948, the rebirth of the modern nation of Israel. Long ago, God promised that those who bless Abraham and his descendants will be blessed and the one who curses them must be cursed (Genesis 12:3). God has never abrogated this promise. Much of America's blessing as a nation can be traced to its benevolent treatment of the Jews and Israel, which has waned dramatically under President Obama. In 2009, he publicly demanded that Israel halt all settlement activity as a condition for further talks with the Palestinians, a demand that the Palestinian negotiator Mahmoud Abbas had not even made. He announced demands on Israel at the UN, contributing to "the atmosphere of menace toward Israel" at the Israel-despising body.[14]

In May 2011, in his most egregious betrayal of Israel, President Obama called on Israel to return to the 1967

borders as the basis for the creation of a neighboring
Palestinian State. This statement put the U.S. squarely
at odds with Israel. Israeli Prime Minister Netanyahu
responded quickly and forthrightly. "While Israel is prepared to make generous compromises for peace, it cannot go back to the 1967 lines. These lines are indefensible.
Remember that, before 1967, Israel was all of nine miles
wide…It was half the width of the Washington Beltway.
And these were not the boundaries of peace; they were
the boundaries of repeated wars, because the attack on
Israel was so attractive."[15] I heard one Israeli official refer
to the 1967 borders as "Auschwitz borders."

One of the surest ways for America to seal its doom
is to turn its back on Israel and force them into a no-win
situation. Again, while support of Israel doesn't mean a
rubber stamp for every policy decision they make, stating
that they must return to the 1967 borders as a condition
for "peace" is a non-starter. As Mona Charen said about
President Obama's posture toward Israel, "A false friend
can do more damage than an open enemy."[16] America must remain a staunch supporter and faithful ally to
Israel. One of the secrets to America's greatness in spite
of all its other failures has been our support of Israel, and
God has blessed America as He promised He would. If
America continues on its current path and fails to bless
the Jewish people, the final vestige of God's blessing
could be withdrawn, and the end could come like a flood.

Pray for our nation!

Pray for our leaders!

CHAPTER SIX

The Coming Middle East Peace

A Temporary Middle East Peace Is on the Horizon

"If an expert says it can't be done, get another expert." [1]

David Ben-Gurion

What is the one issue in our world today that often overshadows all others? What is the one problem that has festered in the world's side for decades? What is the one issue that finds its way into the world's newspapers and television news reports every day? The ongoing hostilities in the Middle East. The Mideast peace process.

The "road map to peace." This one continuing crisis monopolizes world attention.

Have you ever wondered why? Certainly, there are political and humanitarian reasons for the world's interest in this ongoing struggle. But I believe there's more to it than that. The Middle East and its elusive peace process is a key sign of the times. The Bible says that the event that signals the beginning of the final seven-year Tribulation is the signing of a peace treaty or covenant between the leader of the end time Western Confederacy, the final Antichrist, and the nation of Israel (Daniel 9:27). The current turmoil and yearning for peace in the Middle East is setting the stage for the final covenant of peace between Antichrist and Israel predicted in the Bible.

If Israel attacks Iran and a regional war erupts, this could be the final catalyst for this comprehensive peace agreement predicted in Scripture. Syria has endured a bloodbath. Egypt is in chaos and has ushered the Muslim Brotherhood to power. The Palestinians and Hezbollah will be hammered if they retaliate against Israel for striking Iran. After all of this, Israel will be ready for a respite. Israel's neighbors may have been bombed into submission. Iran might even be willing to sign on to some peace agreement to give it time to rearm. The hoofbeats of war we hear today could be the precursor to peace in the future—a peace that's been many years in the making.

The Phantom of Peace

The genesis of the modern peace process in the Middle East really began about ninety years ago. The two main parties in this effort were Emir Faisal, the son of the Sherif of Mecca and Medina, and Chaim Weizmann, the leader of world Zionism, who later became the first president of Israel. These men did forge an agreement in 1918, but it never really got off the ground because of a lack of French and British support.

The peace process has been swimming upstream now for over 60 years. Since the official foundation of Israel as a nation on May 14, 1948, there has been one long war sprinkled with a perpetual peace process between Israel and her Arab neighbors. But there has been no lasting peace. Only brief periods of no war.

The Arab nations surrounding Israel have been in a declared state of war with Israel since May 14, 1948. Only Egypt and Jordan currently have peace with Israel. Here is a brief sketch of the ongoing hostilities between Israel and her neighbors.

| 1948–49 | When Israel officially became an independent state on May 14, 1948, she was immediately attacked from all sides by Egypt, Jordan, Iraq, Syria, Lebanon, and Saudi Arabia. When the truce was implemented on January 7, 1949, Israel had expanded her territory from 5000 square miles to 8000, including much of the Negev, the huge desert to the south between Israel and Egypt. |

1956	The Suez War between Egypt and Israel. Egyptian leader Gamal Abdel Nasser nationalized the Suez Canal. On October 29, 1956, Israel invaded the Sinai Peninsula and took control. Later, Israel returned the Sinai to Egypt.
1964	The Palestinian Liberation Organization (PLO) was formed with the dual purpose of creating a Palestinian State and destroying Israel.
1967	The famous "Six-Day War" (June 5–10). Israel captured the Sinai Peninsula from Egypt, the West Bank from Jordan, the Golan Heights from Syria, and seized control of Jerusalem.
1973	The Yom Kippur War. At 2:00 p.m., on October 6, 1973, on Israel's most holy day, the Day of Atonement (Yom Kippur), Israel was attacked by Egypt and Syria. After heavy fighting, Israel repelled the invaders.
1982–85	The war with Lebanon.
1987–93	The First Palestinian Intifada (uprising) in Gaza. This uprising ended in 1993 with the signing of the Oslo Accords, signed by the prime minister of Israel Yitzhak Rabin and the PLO leader Yasser Arafat.
2000	The Second Palestinian Intifada began in September 2000 when Ariel Sharon visited the Temple Mount. In this uprising, the Palestinians employed suicide (homicide) bombers.
2003	The U.S. presented the "road map" for peace in the Middle East.
2005	Israel withdraws from all 21 settlements in the Gaza Strip.

2006	Israel wages a bloody 34-day War with Hezbollah.
1979–2012	The shadow war between Israel and Iran.

As you can see, the brief history of modern Israel is a history of war, and repeated, futile attempts to grab the phantom of peace. Will a war with Iran be next?

NICE TRY

The United States, the Soviet Union, the United Nations, and various European nations have all given the Middle East peace process their best shot...over and over again. And for the most part, they have failed. In the United States, virtually every president and secretary of state since 1948 has worked at peace, only to come up short again and again. Despite great, well-meaning effort, the world has failed to make any real, lasting headway in the ongoing hostilities between Israel and her neighbors.

The United States was able to broker peace treaties between Israel and her two neighbors, Egypt and Jordan. Nevertheless, both of these nations continue to harbor deep animosity toward Israel, and they often side with other Arab nations in issues involving conflict with Israel. The Oslo Accords, signed on September 13, 1993, on the White House lawn by Yitzhak Rabin and Yasser Arafat, brought great hope. But the second intifada (uprising) that began on September 26, 2000, between Israel and the Palestinians and the 2006 war with Hezbollah in Lebanon and Hamas in Gaza dashed all hopes the Oslo Accords had raised.

Recent events in Egypt (such as the rise of the Muslim Brotherhood to fill the vacuum left by the ousting of Hosni Mubarak) point to a disintegration of the Camp David Accords with Israel. Most Egyptians today want to see the 1979 peace treaty with Israel scrapped.[2] The southern flank of Israel may soon be reopened as a war zone. The showdown with Iran is at its worst. We often wonder if peace will ever come to the Middle East. And what could possibly bring it about?

PEACE IS COMING

A peace treaty for Israel that will be brokered by the coming Antichrist is one of the most important events of the end times. The final Antichrist according to Scripture will rise from a reunited, revived Roman Empire that will probably be centered in Europe. The EU could be the embryonic stages of this power bloc.

The peace treaty he forges will be a false, counterfeit, temporary peace, but it will look like the realization of the world's dream for the Middle East when it is signed.

I believe this treaty will come after the rapture when all believers in Jesus Christ are taken to heaven. This chart helps put the events of the end times in order.

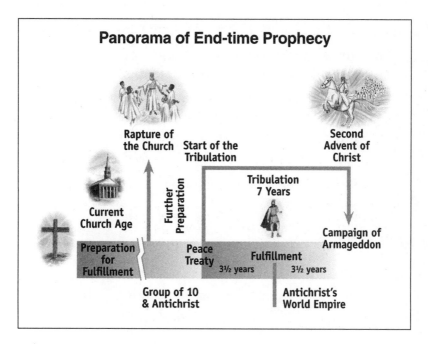

Here is a visual time line that depicts the sequence of events before and during the Tribulation.[3]

Adapted and used with permission of Tim LaHaye and Thomas Ice, *Charting the End Times* (Eugene, OR: Harvest House, 2001). The chart above is based on charts that appear in LaHaye and Ice's book, with one adaptation: the placement of the Group of 10 and Antichrist before the signing of the peace treaty rather than after.

There are two main Old Testament passages that indicate that there will be some kind of peace settlement for Israel at the beginning of the coming seven-year time of Tribulation. I believe that both of these passages refer to the same peace treaty that will be signed at the very beginning of the Tribulation. The first is Daniel 9:27, which says, "And he [Antichrist] will make a firm covenant with the many for one week [7 years], but in the middle of the week he will put a stop to sacrifice and grain offering; and on the wing of abominations will come one who makes desolate." This passage teaches us at least 5 key things about this future peace treaty:

1. It will be between Israel and the Antichrist, but will almost certainly involve others. This seems to indicate that the reunited Roman Empire will be a key player.

2. It will begin the final 7-year time of the Tribulation.

3. It will be a "firm" covenant, which may indicate that it will initially be forced or compelled. It may be a "take it or leave it" deal for Israel and its neighbors.

4. It will eventually give Jews the right to offer sacrifices in a rebuilt temple, which means a Jewish temple must be rebuilt.

5. It will be broken by the Antichrist himself at the midpoint of the treaty in one of the great double-crosses of all time.

Charles Dyer, a respected prophecy teacher and author, summarizes the nature of the Daniel 9:27 covenant:

> What is this "covenant" that the Antichrist will make with Israel? Daniel does not specify its content, but he does indicate that it will extend for seven years. During the first half of this time Israel feels at peace and secure, so the covenant must provide some guarantee for Israel's national security. Very likely the covenant will allow Israel to be at peace with her Arab neighbors. One result of the covenant is that Israel will be allowed to rebuild her temple in Jerusalem. This world ruler will succeed where Kissinger, Carter, Reagan, Bush, and other world leaders have failed. He will be known as the man of peace![4]

The second Old Testament text that speaks of Israel's end-time peace agreement is Ezekiel 38:8, which says that "in the latter years" Israel will be "living securely, all of them." Then verse 11 says that Israel will be "at rest" and will "live securely." According to Ezekiel, there will be a time in the latter years when the regathered people of Israel will be living in a time of great peace and prosperity. During this time, when Israel has let down her guard, a coalition of nations led by Russia and Iran will invade the land and be wiped out by God. We will look at that in more detail in the next chapter. But it's safe to say that what we see today, and have witnessed over the last few decades of the Middle East peace process, points toward this key end-time event that will kick-start the final seven years of this age.

How Much Longer?

What form will the coming peace settlement take? In view of the many surprises, twists, and turns in the Middle East, it is hazardous to guess the precise form of such a final peace settlement. It is also difficult to predict what catastrophic events will make this forced peace necessary. But the outbreak of war as a result of an Israeli preemptive strike against Iran could be the final event that drives the parties to the peace table. It could even be an all-out Middle East war involving the use of tactical nuclear weapons. An Israeli attack against Iran and the Iranian counterstrike through its proxies in Gaza and Lebanon could form part of the backdrop.

Perhaps the conditions in the Middle East will deteriorate so rapidly that a strong military presence will be necessary to restore order. Or perhaps a peace settlement would be accepted by Israel's enemies for a temporary position of advantage in preparation for a possible later war with Israel, as we see in Ezekiel 38–39.

Whatever the reason, the world must be in danger of self-destruction. Otherwise, Israel and the nations of the world would not surrender power to the new leaders of the revived Roman Empire.

Whatever the precipitating events or the form of the peace agreement, ultimately it must give Israel security from attack and freedom from the constant state of military defense. It is very possible that an international peacekeeping force and secure boundaries may be guaranteed by the new and powerful leader of the revived

Roman Empire. A general disarmament in the area may also be part of the agreement. In the aftermath of Israel's indecisive war with Hezbollah in the summer of 2006, Israel was willing to allow a peacekeeping force, led by EU forces, to guarantee the security of its northern border. Israel's agreement to have a U.N. peacekeeping force control southern Lebanon could be a prelude to its willingness to give over more and more of its security to the West.

THE TREATY AND THE TEMPLE

The key issue in negotiations will be the city of Jerusalem itself, which Israel prizes more than any other possession. Undoubtedly there will be a strong attempt to maintain Jerusalem as an international city, with free access not only for Jews but for Christians and Muslims as well. The temple area may be internationalized, and Israel's territorial conquests will be greatly reduced.

With the rise of radical Islamic terrorism and the changing role of the United States as the sole supporting force behind Israel's continuity as a nation, it seems that any settlement that does not deal with Jerusalem will not satisfy the Arab world.

How soon will such a peace settlement come? No one can predict. But come it must—here the Scriptures are emphatic. There will be a treaty between the new world leader and Israel (Daniel 9:27) that will permit Israel to continue and to renew her religious ceremonies, including the building of a Jewish temple and the reactivation of Jewish sacrifices. All of this was anticipated in the prophecies of Daniel 9:27 and 12:11 and was implied in the prophecy of Christ Himself relating to the stopping of the sacrifices when the treaty is broken (Matthew 24:15).

How this temple can be rebuilt is one of the thorniest problems in all of Bible prophecy. How can the Jews rebuild their temple with the Dome of the Rock and the Al-Aqsa mosque sitting there? Many solutions to this problem have been proposed. But never forget that before 1948, people thought it was impossible for the Jewish people to ever be restored to their ancient homeland. Yet, today almost 40 percent of the Jews in the world now live in Israel, and incredibly almost two-thirds of them now want to see the temple rebuilt.

Ynetnews reported the startling findings of a new poll about the temple on July 30, 2009. The poll asked respondents whether they wanted to see the temple rebuilt:

> Sixty-four percent responded favorably, while 36% said no. An analysis of the answers showed that not only the ultra-Orthodox and the religious look forward to the rebuilding of the Temple (100% and 97% respectively), but also the traditional public (91%) and many seculars—47%…The Temple was destroyed 1,942 years ago, and almost two-thirds of the population want to see it rebuilt, including 47% of seculars.

This ground swell of support for a third Jewish temple is another key sign of the times. For years, groups like the temple Mount Faithful and others have championed and even made preparations for the rebuilding of the temple, but broad public support seemed woefully lacking. That appears to have drastically changed. The temple must be in place during the Tribulation period for the Antichrist to take his seat in it and defile it as predicted in 2 Thessalonians 2:4 and for sacrifices to be reinstituted.

While no one knows when it will be rebuilt or how it will be accomplished, the stage setting for its appearance and the coming treaty of peace continues to fall into place. The Israel-Iran showdown may be a critical cog in the wheel that brings the nations to the bargaining table for a comprehensive Middle East peace.

CHAPTER SEVEN

The Ezekiel Prophecy

Bible Prophecy Predicts a Future Middle East War

*"Great events in history often gather momentum
and power long before they are recognized by
the experts and commentators on world affairs.
Easily one of the most neglected but powerfully
galvanizing forces shaping history in the world
today is the prophecy of Gog and Magog from the
38th and 39th chapters of the book of Ezekiel."* [1]

Jon Mark Ruthven,
The Prophecy That Is Shaping History

A s you read these words, Israel and Iran are squaring
off in a death struggle that points toward what the
Bible predicts for the end times in the ancient prophecy
found in Ezekiel 38–39. Everything that's been presented

in this book up to this point strikingly foreshadows this prophecy.

These chapters, written almost 2600 years ago, describe a great coalition of nations, including Iran, that will invade the land of Israel when Israel is regathered and resting in her land in the latter years. It prophesies a great end-time conflagration commonly called the Battle of Gog and Magog. This will be the first of two great end-time wars. Before you read this chapter, it would be helpful to turn to appendix 3 and read Ezekiel 38–39 to familiarize yourself with these chapters.

To help us unpack this great prophecy and its meaning for today, I want to focus on four key points: the Allies, the Activities, the Annihilation, and the Aftermath.

THE ALLIES

Ezekiel 38 opens with a list of the nations that will constitute the invading force that will attack Israel in the end times:

> And the word of the LORD came to me saying, "Son of man, set your face toward Gog of the land of Magog, the prince of Rosh, Meshech and Tubal, and prophesy against him and say, 'Thus says the Lord GOD, "Behold, I am against you, O Gog, prince of Rosh, Meshech and Tubal. I will turn you about and put hooks into your jaws, and I will bring you out, and all your

army, horses and horsemen, all of them splendidly attired, a great company with buckler and shield, all of them wielding swords; Persia, Ethiopia and Put with them, all of them with shield and helmet; Gomer with all its troops; Beth-togarmah from the remote parts of the north with all its troops—many peoples with you. Be prepared, and prepare yourself, you and all your companies that are assembled about you, and be a guard for them"'" (Ezekiel 38:1-7).

None of the place names in Ezekiel 38:1-7 exist on any modern map. Ezekiel used ancient place names that were familiar to the people of his day. While the names of these geographical locations have changed many times throughout history and may change again, the geographical territory remains the same. Regardless of what names they may carry at the time of this invasion, it is these specific geographical areas that will be involved, as Thomas Ice points out:

It appears that Ezekiel is using the names of peoples, primarily from the table of nations, and where they lived at the time of the giving of this prophecy in the sixth century B.C. Therefore, if we are able to find out where these people and places were in the sixth century B.C. then we will be able to...figure out who would be their modern antecedents today.[2]

Let's examine each of the ancient names to discover the modern counterparts that will participate in this last days' invasion of Israel.

GOG

The first name that appears is "Gog." This name is used eleven times in Ezekiel 38–39. From the context of Ezekiel, it's clear that Gog is the leader of this invasion and that Gog is an individual. He is directly addressed several times by God (38:14; 39:1) and is called a prince (38:2; 39:1). The word "Gog" means "height or mountain" and probably refers to the pride and arrogance of this leader.

Many believe that Gog is the same person as the Antichrist. I don't agree with this view. I believe the Antichrist will lead the Western confederacy of the end times, while Gog will lead a Russian–Islamic coalition. Gog and the Antichrist will be enemies vying for power against one another.

MAGOG

The ancient Scythians inhabited the land of Magog.[3] The Scythians were fierce, northern nomadic tribes who inhabited territory that stretches today from Central Asia across the southern steppes of modern Russia. Modern Magog probably represents the former underbelly of the Soviet Union: Kazakhstan, Kirghizia, Uzbekistan, Turkmenistan, and Tajikistan. Russia could also be included in Magog as well as Afghanistan. All of these nations, other than Russia, are dominated by Islam, with a combined total population in excess of sixty million.

ROSH

Bible scholars have often identified Rosh in Ezekiel 38:2 with Russia. There is strong linguistic, historical evidence for making this connection.[4] Ezekiel predicts that the great Russian bear will rise in the last days to mount a furious invasion of Israel. The prophet Ezekiel predicted 2600 years ago that in the latter times Israel would be invaded by a people "from the distant north" or "remotest parts of the north" (38:6,15; 39:2). The nation to the distant or far north of Israel is Russia. Many mistakenly thought that when the Soviet Union was dissolved, the great Russian bear went into permanent hibernation. But the Russian bear today is a much more dangerous bear than ever before. The mighty Soviet Union has been dissolved—Russia has been left as a mother bear robbed of her cubs.

The fulfillment of God's prophecies concerning Russia seem more imminent than ever before. As we track the bear in the end times, we discover that her footprints lead right to the land of Israel. The preliminary setup for this invasion could be developing right before our eyes. Current events bear a remarkable correspondence to biblical prophecies.

Think about it. If Israel is forced to take out the Iranian nuclear megaplex soon, this will sow seeds of vitriolic hatred against Israel in Iran that could precipitate the Gog invasion in the near future. It could serve as the explosive catalyst for the nations in the Gog coalition to begin a plot for an all-out attack—a final payback against Israel. Such a strike could even be the "hooks in the jaws" that draw Russia into the fray. Russia has repeatedly warned Israel not to attack Iran.

General Jerry Boykin, a retired three star general and former Undersecretary of Defense for Intelligence has offered this perspective:

> If Israel were to strike Iran...you would see it accelerate the relationship between Russia and Iran. I think Russia would then come to the aid of...the Iranians and I think you would see that relationship solidify with increased military cooperation and military support, the sale of additional military equipment and even military advice. And that sets the stage for ultimately what is described in Ezekiel 38 and 39.[5]

Things are clearly in a state of flux right now, but the Bible is clear where it's all headed and what will ultimately transpire.

It's very possible that something like the scenario we see unfolding today could be the "hooks in the jaws" that God uses to pull a reluctant Russia down into the land of Israel in the latter years. Russia's geopolitical strategy to deepen its relationship with Iran and other Muslim nations could very well be what will pull them into Israel in the end times as Ezekiel predicted.

Prophecy expert Thomas Ice envisions this kind of future scenario:

> I could see the Muslims coming to the Russians and telling them that America has set a precedent for an outside power coming into the Middle East to right a perceived wrong. (America has done it again in recent years by going into Afghanistan and Iraq.) On that basis, Russia should help out her Muslim friends by leading them in an overwhelming invasion of Israel in order to solve the Middle East Conflict in favor of the Islamic nations. Will this be the "hook in the jaw" of Gog? Only time will tell. But something is up in the Middle East and Russia appears to have her fingerprints all over things. We know that the Bible predicts just such an alignment and invasion to take place "in the latter years." [6]

Russia has a vital stake in Iran. The leadership of Russia, under Vladimir Putin, has carefully protected its interests in Iran and has consistently shielded Iran from any serious action by the U.N. Security Council:

> The pivotal consideration in Mr. Putin's efforts to re-establish his country's superpower status

centers on Iran. Syria is a domino. Without its Syrian ally, Iran would be almost totally isolated and crucially weakened. That Moscow cannot allow. Why is Iran so central to Mr. Putin's global pretensions? Take a look at the Caspian Sea area map and the strategic equations come into relief. Iran acts as a southern bottleneck to the geography of Central Asia. It could offer the West access to the region's resources that would bypass Russia. If Iran reverted to pro-Western alignment, the huge reserves of oil and gas land-locked in Kazakhstan and Turkmenistan and the like could flow directly out to the world without a veto from Moscow...At stake here is not merely the liberation of a vast landmass from the Kremlin's yoke. The damage to Russian leverage would amount to a seismic shift in the global balance of power equal to the collapse of the Warsaw Pact. Russia's gas and oil lever-age over Turkey, Ukraine and much of Europe would evaporate.[7]

Putin cannot allow the mystique of Russian power to deflate. Iran is the centerpiece of that image. Russian ties with Iran have become very cozy in recent days. Massive joint military exercises involving Iran, Russia, China, and Syria point toward a coming war. Iran, Russia, China, and Syria conducted a joint military exercise in the Middle East. Some 90,000 troops from the four countries participated in land, air, and sea maneuvers off the Syrian coast, including air defense and missile units. Additionally, about 400 warplanes and 1000 tanks took part in the exercise. Egypt granted authorization for 12 Chinese warships to sail through the Suez Canal. Russian atomic submarines, warships, aircraft carriers, and Iranian battle ships docked at Syrian ports. During the exercise, Syria tested its air defense systems and coast-to-sea missiles. Two Russian amphibious landing vessels landed at the Russian base at the Syrian port of Tartus.[8] The current close ties between Russia and Iran point toward the biblical prophecy in Ezekiel 38–39.

MESHECH AND TUBAL

Meshech and Tubal are normally mentioned together in Scripture. They are listed two other times in Ezekiel (27:13; 32:26). The preferred identification is that Meshech and Tubal are the ancient Moschoi and Tibarenoi in Greek writings or Tabal and Musku in Assyrian inscriptions. The ancient locations are in present-day Turkey. This is best understood as a reference to modern Turkey, an Islamic country that is currently moving away from Israel and more and more toward its Islamic neighbors.

PERSIA

The ancient land of Persia became the modern nation of Iran in March 1935, and then the name was changed to the Islamic Republic of Iran in 1979. Iran's present population is about 80 million. Iran's regime is the world's number one sponsor of terror. Iran is making its bid for regional supremacy at the same time it is pursuing nuclear weapons.

Ethiopia (Cush)

The Hebrew word Cush in Ezekiel 38:5 is often translated "Ethiopia" in modern versions. Ancient Cush was called Kusu by the Assyrians and Babylonians, Kos or Kas by the Egyptians, and Nubia by the Greeks. Secular history locates Cush directly south of ancient Egypt extending down past the modern city of Khartoum, which is the capital of modern Sudan. Thus, modern Sudan inhabits the ancient land of Cush. Sudan has recently divided. Northern Sudan is a hard-line Islamic nation that supported Iraq in the Gulf War and harbored Osama bin Laden from 1991 to 1996. It is not surprising that this part of Africa would be hostile to the West and could easily join in an attack on Israel.

Southern Sudan, which is mostly Christian, became Africa's fifty-fourth nation in July 2011. A referendum for independence in January 2011 was approved by an almost unanimous vote. The division of the nation into the Islamic north and mostly Christian south is another move that makes the fulfillment of the Ezekiel prophecy even more likely since the radical Islamic north will now be able to act on its own.

In light of the independence of southern Sudan, the Sudanese President Omar al Bashir stated that North Sudan will intensify its adherence to Sharia law:

If the south Sudan secedes, we will change the constitution and at that time there will be no time to speak of diversity of culture and ethnicity. Sharia (Islamic law) and Islam will be the main source for the constitution, Islam the official religion and Arabic the official language.[9]

North Sudan is poised to take its place in the coming Gog alliance just as Ezekiel predicted.

LIBYA (PUT)

Ancient sources locate Put or Phut in North Africa. The Babylonian Chronicles, which are a series of tablets recording ancient Babylonian history, states that Put was the "distant" land to the west of Egypt, which would be modern-day Libya and could possibly include nations further west such as modern Algeria and Tunisia. The Septuagint, which was the Greek translation of the Old Testament, renders the word Put as Libues.

Modern Libya, an Islamic nation, suffered under the rule of Colonel Muammar al-Gadhafi from 1969 until the revolution in 2011. The madman was finally ousted, but the transition to another government has been rocky, to say the least.

In the wake of the revolution, many fear a fragmented nation will emerge. Eastern Libya, where the country's oil fields are located, has threatened to seek a semiautonomous existence and eventually form a separate eastern state. The central government has proved itself incapable of governing at all. Hope is dying:

> After the liberation from the rule of Gadhafi, Libyans dreamed their country of 6 million could become another Dubai—a state with a small population, flush with petro-dollars, that is a magnet for investment. Now they worry that it is turning more into another Somalia, a nation with no effective government for more than 20 years.[10]

Libya appears headed for years of instability. Islamic jihadists, acting like vigilantes, attacked shrines and monuments deemed un-Islamic. The Muslim Brotherhood, which was banned during Gadhafi's reign, has formed a political party in Libya called the Justice and Development Party. When the dust finally settles in Libya, the nation could find itself in the clutches of radical Islamic leaders that could jump at the chance to be part of a coalition to invade Israel.

GOMER

Gomer refers to the ancient Cimmerians or Kimmerioi. Ancient history identifies biblical Gomer with the Akkadian Gi-mir-ra-a and the Armenian Gamir. Beginning in the eighth century BC, the Cimmerians occupied territory in Anatolia, which is modern Turkey. Josephus noted that the Gomerites were identified with the

Galatians, who inhabited what today is central Turkey.[11] Turkey is an Islamic nation with deepening ties with Russia. Turkey's natural allegiance is not with the EU but to her Muslim neighbors.

BETH-TOGARMAH

Beth-togarmah means the "house of Togarmah." Togarmah is mentioned in Ezekiel 27:14 as a nation that traded horses and mules with ancient Tyre. Ancient Togarmah was also known as Til-garamu (Assyrian) or Tegarma (Hittite) and its territory is in modern Turkey, which is north of Israel. Again, Turkey is identified as part of this group of nations that attack Israel.

THE END-TIME GOG COALITION	
Rosh (ancient Rashu, Rasapu, Ros, and Rus)	Russia
Magog (ancient Scythians)	Central Asia
Meshech (ancient Muschki and Musku)	Turkey
Tubal (ancient Tubalu)	Turkey
Persia	Iran
Ethiopia (Cush)	Sudan

Put or Phut	Libya
Gomer (ancient Cimmerians)	Turkey
Beth-togarmah (ancient Til-garimmu or Tegarma)	Turkey

Many of these nations are either forming or strengthening their ties as these words are being written. This list of nations reads like the Who's Who of this week's newspaper. It's not too difficult to imagine these nations, all of whom are Islamic other than Russia, conspiring together to invade Israel in the near future, especially if Israel launches a preemptive strike against Iran.

Of course, the Bible never mentions Islam, since Islam was not founded until the seventh century AD, and the New Testament was completed in AD 95. However, isn't it interesting that all the nations in Ezekiel 38:1-7 that attack Israel in the end times are currently Islamic nations with the exception of Russia? And most of them are currently avowed enemies of Israel (Persia, Libya, and Sudan). There is nothing that these nations would love more than to invade Israel to wipe her off the face of the earth. Obviously, God knew this when Ezekiel penned his prophecy in about 570 BC, proving once again that the Bible is divine in origin.

THE PROTESTERS

Everything we see today suggests that Iran and the other nations in Ezekiel 39 are on a collision course with Israel and would gladly join with the Gog alliance of Ezekiel 38 when it comes together. However, we have to remember that there's also a sizable rift between Iran and the Sunni nations such as Saudi Arabia and the Gulf States. This corresponds to the picture presented in Ezekiel 38–39 as well. When Russia, Central Asia, Iran, Turkey, North Sudan, and Libya (and possibly other nations) join together to assault Israel, a group of other nations sit on the sidelines, offering a lame protest to what's happening. This protest is recorded in Ezekiel 38:10-13.

> Thus says the Lord GOD, "It will come about on that day, that thoughts will come into your mind and you will devise an evil plan, and you will say, 'I will go up against the land of unwalled villages. I will go against those who are at rest, that live securely, all of them living without walls and having no bars or gates, to capture spoil and to seize plunder, to turn your hand against the waste places which are now inhabited, and against the people who are gathered from the nations, who have acquired cattle and goods, who live at the center of the world.' Sheba and Dedan and the merchants of Tarshish with all its villages will say to you, 'Have you come to capture spoil? Have you assembled

> your company to seize plunder, to carry away
> silver and gold, to take away cattle and goods,
> to capture great spoil?'"

The nations that lodge this objection are identified as "Sheba, Dedan and the merchants of Tarshish with all its villages." Sheba and Dedan are the current nations we know as Saudi Arabia and the more moderate Gulf States. These nations, which are Sunni Muslims, are strongly opposed to Iran and its nuclear quest. It's no stretch to see them standing on the sidelines offering dissent to this future invasion. The actions of Sheba and Dedan also fit what we see today.

The reference to "the merchants of Tarshish with all its villages" is not as easy to identify. Three ancient places were known as "Tarshish." First, there was a place with this name on the east coast of Africa, although the exact location is not known.[12] Second, another Tarshish was located in England. Third, a place known as Tartessus was in the present-day nation of Spain. The weight of authority seems to favor the third view. This was the view of the Hebrew scholar Heinrich Friedrich Wilhelm Gesenius.[13] In biblical times, Tarshish was a wealthy, flourishing Phoenician colony located in modern Spain which exported silver, iron, tin, and lead (Jeremiah 10:9; Ezekiel 27:12,25).

According to the New American Standard Bible (NASB), Ezekiel also refers to "the merchants of Tarshish with all its villages" (38:13). Compare the translation offered by the New International Version (NIV): "the merchants of Tarshish and all her villages." But the translation presented by the King James Version (KJV) is probably the best: "Tarshish with all the young lions thereof." Young lions are often used in Scripture to refer to powerful, energetic rulers. Therefore, the young lions who join with Tarshish to verbally oppose Gog's invasion could be strong military and political leaders who act in concert with Tarshish.

Another possibility is that the phrase "all the young lions"—or "all its villages," as the NASB has it—refers to the nations that have come out of or originated from Tarshish.[14] If this is correct, the question again is, where was Tarshish in Ezekiel's day? Apparently, it was in the farthest western regions of the known world, which would be located in Spain.

Jonah was commanded by God to go preach to Nineveh (about 500 miles northeast of Israel). But Jonah headed as far in the opposite direction as he could go, which was to Tarshish (Jonah 1:1-3). Spain, of course, is in modern Europe. More specifically, it is in Western Europe. Tarshish, or modern Spain, may be used by Ezekiel to refer to the nations of Western Europe who will join the moderate Arab states in denouncing this invasion. Tarshish is often associated with the far West in Scripture: "The western kings of Tarshish and other distant lands will bring him tribute" (Psalm 72:10 NLT).

The young lions of Tarshish could be a reference to the colonies that emerged from Europe, including the

United States. If this is true, then the young lions of Tarshish describe the United States in the last days joining in with her European and Saudi-Gulf State allies to lodge a formal protest against the Russian-Islamic aggressors. If Tarshish was in England, then the "young lions thereof" could refer to "the United States, Canada, Australia, New Zealand, and other present-day western democracies" that came from England.[15] This would be a clear biblical reference to the role of America in the end times. However, this lone reference seems too tenuous for me to fully get on board with this view.

Nevertheless, whether you take these young lions to refer to the United States or to the Western powers of the last days, the scenario that is presented in Ezekiel 38 fits the present world political situation to a tee. Russia continues to flex its muscle in the Middle East by forging alliances with Iran and Arab nations. The Islamic nations of ancient Magog (Central Asia) are developing and deepening ties with Iran, Russia, and Turkey. The hatred for Israel by the Middle East Muslim nations continues to fester and boil. It's not too difficult to imagine the nations mentioned in Ezekiel 38:1-7 coming together under Russian leadership to mount a furious attack against Israel. It's also not difficult to imagine the Western powers of the last days objecting to the attack.

The Near Enemies

Ezekiel 38 lists what is often described as the "far enemies" of Israel. If you look on a map, you will see that the nations listed are the farthest enemies of Israel in every direction: Russia to the north, Iran to the east, Sudan to the south, and Libya to the west. This raises an important question: What will happen to the near enemies of Israel, such as Jordan, Egypt, Gaza, Syria, and Lebanon? They aren't mentioned in Ezekiel 38. Does the Bible say anything about the fate of these nations?

Some commentators have answered this question by taking Psalm 83, which lists the main near enemies of Israel, and viewing it as a separate war that will precede the war in Ezekiel 38–39 and will dispose of Israel's near enemies. They believe that the destruction of Israel's near enemies, which they often call the Psalm 83 War, will pave the way for the rest and security that Israel will enjoy (Ezekiel 38:8,11). While this scenario could be correct, I prefer to see Psalm 83 as similar to Psalm 2 and not as a separate end-time war.

Psalm 2 highlights the age-long hatred and conspiracy of the nations against the Lord and His anointed One, the Messiah. The similarities with Psalm 83 are apparent. Nations are conspiring against the Lord and the Davidic King.

The Lord scoffs at them and predicts a time when (1) they will be destroyed, (2) His King will rule the earth, and (3) people will submit to Him. This looks ahead to the messianic kingdom or 1000-year reign of Christ, which brings the end times to a head. The main difference between these two passages is that Psalm 2 does not specifically enumerate the nations, but Psalm 83 lists ten specific enemies.

Nevertheless, the point is the same. The enemies of God and His anointed King will one day be destroyed and will submit to Him. People don't look for some separate "Psalm 2 War." Instead, they see it as a general prophecy that the Lord's enemies will be destroyed in the end times. I believe that's the same thing that's going on in Psalm 83.

We have to remember that the Psalms were written long before the prophets began to write and give specific prophecies concerning the nations. The prophets are where we look to find specific prophecies concerning the nations and end-time events. The Psalms certainly do contain messianic prophecies, but I'm not aware of other specific, detailed prophecies in the Psalms concerning the Gentile nations in the end times.

I believe that constructing a separate end-time war out of Psalm 83 is reading too much into a text that is simply saying that Israel has been and always will be surrounded by enemies and that someday the Lord will finally deal with them. In Psalm 83, God is bolstering and encouraging the nation and its king at the very beginning of the Davidic reign, promising that He will ultimately prevail over His enemies and will protect His people from extinction.

So what will happen to Israel's near enemies? It could be that the Bible simply doesn't tell us about their immediate fate. Or they could be included in the Battle of Gog and Magog. The mention of the far circle of nations around Israel could include the near nations as well.

After all, the final words of Ezekiel 38:6 are "many peoples with you." This could be a catch-all to include other nations not specifically mentioned in Ezekiel 38:6, and some of the near enemies of Israel could be included in this description.

ISLAM AND EZEKIEL 38–39

Ironically, Islam has its own version of the Battle of Gog and Magog called the War of Yajuj and Majuj, but it's very different from the biblical account. In two places, the Quran specifically mentions "Gog and Magog" (Yajuj and Majuj) by name (18:96; 21:96). Islamic eschatology teaches that there are ten major signs that signal the approach of the end and the day of resurrection. There are various opinions about the order of these signs, but in at least one list, Gog and Magog is the number four sign.

According to Islamic teaching, Gog and Magog are two groups of Turks that were spreading corruption through the earth during the time of Abraham. Finally, to keep them in check, they were enclosed behind a great barrier. They tried in vain to climb over it and have been trying to dig under the wall for centuries, but they will not be able to get out until Allah decrees that they can be released. Then, the barrier will collapse, and Gog and Magog will pour out in all directions, rushing into the land of Israel to attack the Muslims there. When Jesus prays against Gog and Magog, Allah will wipe them out by means of some kind of disease or plague that he will send upon them. The disease is described as either infectious, lethal boils, or a disease that eats the flesh from their bones.

If that sounds familiar, it should. It was evidently taken by Muhammad straight from Ezekiel 38, with a few convenient changes to fit his own ends. Ezekiel 38:22 specifically says that God will destroy the invaders with pestilence and with blood. Therefore, while Muslims believe in the prophecy of Gog and Magog, they appear to be totally ignorant of the fact that all the nations that will be destroyed by God in Ezekiel 38 are Muslim nations today, with the exception of Russia. One of their ten great signs of the end will actually be fulfilled by them when they attack Israel in the last days.

THE ACTIVITY

Ezekiel says that these nations led by Russia, and with Iran as key participant, will come against Israel "after many days" at a time when the people of Israel are living in peace ("at rest," "securely") and prosperity (38:8-12). The timing of this invasion is the most debated issue. It has been placed at about every point in time in the latter years. Many excellent prophecy teachers believe the battle of Gog and Magog could occur before the rapture happens or at least before the Tribulation period begins. Proponents of this view believe the Gog-Magog War could happen at any time, which certainly adds a sense of urgency to what's transpiring today. While this view is certainly possible, Ezekiel says the invasion occurs in the "last days" or "latter years" for Israel, which I believe begin with the Tribulation period. For this reason, I don't believe it can happen before that time.

Others equate this invasion with the Campaign of Armageddon that will transpire at the end of the Tribulation period. The main support for this view is that both events are attended by a great bird supper feeding on the carnage (Ezekiel 39:4-5,17-20; Revelation 19:17-18). Although this similarity is noteworthy, it's not unusual that two different wars could each include a feasting by the birds. The primary problem with this view is that Israel will not be at rest at the conclusion of the Tribulation. Israel will have endured three-and-a-half years of persecution by the Antichrist by that time, so the peace prerequisite for the invasion will not be present.

All things considered, I believe this invasion will transpire during the first half of the coming seven-year Tribulation, when Israel will be living under her peace treaty with Antichrist. Ezekiel repeatedly emphasizes that when this invasion occurs, Israel will be back in the land "living securely" (38:8,11,14) and "at rest" (38:11). Although some would argue that Israel today is "living securely" and "at rest," I believe that's quite a stretch when one looks at the current situation in Israel.

The language in Ezekiel 38 seems to fit best during the first half of the coming seven-year Tribulation. However, one should avoid dogmatism concerning the timing of this invasion, and here's why: Excellent prophecy teachers disagree about this aspect of the prophecy. All we can say for sure about it is that it's future. No event in the past even comes close to fulfilling the events described in Ezekiel 38–39.

What we know for sure is that sometime in the future this invasion will occur. When the massive foray into Israel occurs, Russia and her Islamic allies will descend upon the nation of Israel "like a storm" and "will be like a cloud covering the land" (38:9). From the text of Ezekiel and parallel Old Testament passages, there are four main reasons why Russia and her allies will invade Israel.

1. *To cash in on the wealth of Israel (Ezekiel 38:11-12).* The exact nature of this wealth is never specifically stated, but some people speculate that it could involve the vast oil and gas reserves that are currently being discovered and tapped in Israel. A gargantuan deposit of natural gas was discovered off Israel's Mediterranean coast in December 2010, and an even larger area of shale oil has been found near Jerusalem. It's believed this will turn Israel into a net exporter of oil and gas. The Arabs in the Middle East no longer have a monopoly on energy.

2. *To control the Middle East.* While this is not specifically stated in the text, one can assume that this would be part of any invasion of this magnitude.

3. *To crush Israel.* The Islamic nations mentioned in Scripture hate Israel and would love nothing

more than to "come like a storm" and "like a cloud covering the land." This invasion will look like the long-awaited fulfillment of the Muslim dream to drive the Jews into the sea.

4. *To challenge the authority of Antichrist.* If I'm correct about the timing of this invasion during the first half of the Tribulation, Israel will be under her peace treaty with Antichrist at the time of this attack.

Therefore, the attack against Israel (the battle of Gog and Magog) will represent a direct challenge by Russia and its Islamic allies to Antichrist and the West. After the armies of Ezekiel 38 are destroyed by God, Antichrist will break his covenant with Israel and invade the land himself (Daniel 11:41-44). The destruction of the Russian-Islamic army will leave a gaping power vacuum that the Antichrist will also quickly move to fill, eventually establishing his one-world government and economy at the midpoint of the seven-year Tribulation. He will rule the world for the final three-and-a-half years of the age.

THE ANNIHILATION OF THE INVADERS

When these nations invade the land of Israel, it will look like the biggest military mismatch in history. It will make the invasions of Israel in 1967 and 1973 by the Arab nations pale in comparison. When this last days strike force sweeps into the land, it will look like Israel is finished forever. But God is in control of the entire situation. He will mount up in His fury to destroy these godless invaders: "'It will come about on that day, when Gog invades the land of Israel,' declares the Lord GOD, 'that My fury will mount up in My anger! In My zeal and in My blazing wrath…'" (Ezekiel 39:18-19).

God will come to rescue His helpless people and will use these means to destroy Russia and her allies:

1. He will send a great earthquake (38:19-20).

2. There will be infighting among the troops of the various nations (38:21). In the chaotic aftermath of the powerful earthquake, the armies of each of the nations represented will turn against each other. This will be the largest case of death by friendly fire in human history.

3. The invaders will also experience dreadful disease (38:22).

4. God will send torrential rain, hailstones, fire, and burning sulfur (38:22).

The famous Six-Day War occurred in Israel in June, 1967. This will be the "One-Day War" (or even the "One-Hour War"), when God supernaturally destroys this Russian-Islamic horde.

THE AFTERMATH OF THE WAR

Four key events will unfold in the aftermath of this invasion.

1. *The birds and the beasts (Ezekiel 39:4-5,17-20; cf. Revelation 19:17-18).* The carnage that results from this slaughter will provide a great feast for the birds of the air and the beasts of the field. God refers to the carnage as "my sacrificial feast" and "my banquet table" to which He invites the birds and the beasts as His guests.

2. *The seven-month burying of the dead (Ezekiel 39:11-12,14-16).* Clean-up squads will be assembled to go through the land. They will set up markers wherever they see a human bone. When the gravediggers come behind them they will see the markers and take the remains to the Valley of Gog's Hordes for burial. The cleansing will be so extensive that a town will be established in the valley at the gravesites to aid those who are cleansing the land. The name of the town will be Hamonah (horde).

3. *The seven-year burning of the weapons (Ezekiel 39:9-10).* Since the battle of Gog and Magog occurs during the first half of the Tribulation, the Israelites will continue to burn these

weapons on into the millennial kingdom for three-and-a-half years.

4. *The blessing of salvation (Ezekiel 39:25-29).* In the midst of His wrath and fury, God will also pour out His grace and mercy. God will use the awesome display of His power against the invading armies to bring many to salvation of both Jews and Gentiles.

God makes it clear that He will have the last word:

> "I will bring you against my land as everyone watches, and my holiness will be displayed by what happens to you, Gog. Then all the nations will know that I am the LORD...I will make myself known to all the nations of the world. Then they will know that I am the LORD...Then they will know that I am the LORD. In this way, I will make known my holy name among my people of Israel. I will not let anyone bring shame on it. And all the nations, too, will know that I am the LORD, the Holy One of Israel... In this way, I will demonstrate my glory to the nations...And from that time on the people of Israel will know that I am the LORD their God" (Ezekiel 38:16,23; 39:6-7,21,22 NLT).

Many of those who turn to the true God as a result of this demonstration of His power will undoubtedly be among the vast group of the redeemed in Revelation 7:9-14.

Conclusion

Over and over again in Ezekiel 38–39, God makes it clear that He is in charge. If there's one thing we learn from Ezekiel 38–39 above all else, it's that God is in control. He says to these future invaders, "And I will turn you about and put hooks into your jaws, and I will bring you out" (38:4). God pictures these invading nations as a huge crocodile that He drags out of the water.

In Ezekiel 38–39, seven times we read the same words: "Thus says the Lord God" (38:3,10,14,17; 39:1,17,25). Another eight times this refrain appears: "declares the Lord God" (38:18,21; 39:5,8,10,13,20,29). Obviously, God doesn't want us to miss the point—this is His Word. The prediction in Ezekiel 38–39 comes directly from Him. He is the author of the script.

In other places, God further emphasizes that He is sovereignly at work in human affairs:

- "You will be summoned" (38:8).

- "I will bring you against My land" (38:16).

- "I will turn you around, drive you on, take you up…and bring you against the mountains of Israel" (39:2).

Obviously, God is not violating the will of these invaders by bringing them into Israel. They want to come. They "devise an evil plan," and God holds them responsible for it (38:10). Nothing in this statement is meant in any way to lessen human responsibility. The point is that God is ultimately and finally in control. He's the director. He is the one who is making sure the stage is perfectly set for His great prophetic production.

God has scripted many events and participants to play certain roles in His prophetic production, but as we have seen, one of the major events that God has scripted for the end times is the Battle of Gog and Magog. It is the first major military campaign of the end times.

The rise of militant Islam has shocked and surprised most people. But 2600 years ago, God amazingly predicted through the prophet Ezekiel the exact scenario that we see developing before our eyes every day on the evening news.

Ezekiel 36–39 is "history written beforehand." Ezekiel 36–37 describes the regathering of Jews to the land of Israel in the end times. Then this regathering is followed by an all-out invasion of Israel by a massive assault force in Ezekiel 38–39. On May 14, 1948, Israel became a nation against all odds, preparing the way for the first part of Ezekiel's prophecy to be fulfilled. As we look around today, it appears that the stage is being set for the rest of his prophecy to come to pass exactly as God predicted.

All the nations in Ezekiel 38 are identifiable countries with the will and desire to eliminate Israel. Many of these nations are forming alliances with one another. The crisis between Iran and Israel has reached a boiling point that could spill over to the entire Middle East, toppling dominos that will further pave the way for this predicted war.

The world is yearning for peace in the Middle East, and this peace will bring about the rest and security that must exist for this invasion to occur.

In all of this, Iran is a key place to watch. We see events in Iran and places all over the Middle East splashed across the television screen and news headlines every day, and they are like runway lights beginning to light up as the coming of Christ approaches.

CHAPTER EIGHT

The Times of the Signs

Current Developments Strikingly Foreshadow the End of Days

"The study of history and prophecy as it relates to the nations is especially appropriate at this point in the twentieth century when history seems to be moving rapidly toward its destiny. Only the divine interpretation of history and the divine revelation of the prophetic future of nations can give us a sure light in these troubled times."[1]

John F. Walvoord, *The Nations in Prophecy* (1967)

Some signs are easier to read than others. This is especially true when traveling to a foreign country. Meaning often gets "lost in translation." Here are a few signs in other countries translated into English:

In a Paris elevator: "Please leave your values at the front desk."

In a hotel in Athens: "Visitors are expected to complain at the office between the hours of 9 and 11 a.m. daily."

In an Austrian hotel catering to skiers: "Not to perambulate the corridors during the hours of repose in the boots of ascension."

In a Rhodes tailor shop: "Order your summers suit. Because is a big rush we will execute customers in strict rotation."

In an advertisement by a Hong Kong dentist: "Teeth extracted by the latest Methodists."

In a Copenhagen airline ticket office: "We take your bags and send them in all directions." [Yes, they do!]

In an Acapulco hotel: "The manager has personally passed all the water served here."

In a Tokyo shop: "Our nylons cost more than common, but you'll find they are best in the long run."[2]

It's true. Some signs are clearer than others. Some are straightforward and easy to read, while others are more difficult. Jesus chided the people in His day for failing to discern the signs of the times of His first advent (Matthew 16:1-3). He told us that clear signs will portend His second advent (Matthew 24:4-31; Luke 21:25).

Make no mistake. The prophecies of the Bible will be fulfilled. Just as hundreds of past prophecies have been literally fulfilled just as the Bible predicted, we know that the unfulfilled prophecies will also literally come to pass. The Bible has a proven track record. The only question is—*when* will God bring them to pass? We can watch today as the various players assume their roles and the necessary scenes move into place on the set. We can watch the buildup as it happens.

WHAT TO WATCH FOR

In the pages of Scripture, God has given us some "signs of the times" that are clear if we will look for them. What are some of these signs we should be looking for? Which events on the horizon today point toward what lies ahead? Let me mention five specific signposts on the road to the Battle of Gog and Magog and beyond.

The Regathering of Israel

One unmistakable sign is the rebirth of the modern state of Israel and the regathering of the Jewish people to their ancient homeland. Since 1948, this signpost has been in place. This is often referred to as the super sign of the end times, since so many other end-time prophecies hinge on the presence of the Jewish people in their land. Israel is at the center of God's end-time agenda. Almost 40 percent of the Jews in the world now live in Israel. The hundreds of ancient prophecies about the end-time restoration of the Jewish people to their land are coming to fruition before our eyes. This piece of the prophetic puzzle must be in place for the end times to commence, and it has been in place for over 60 years.

The Reuniting of the Roman Empire

The Scriptures predict in Daniel 2 and 7 and Revelation 13 and 17 that the Roman Empire will be revived or reunited in the end times. It will begin as a confederation of nations ruled over by ten kings or leaders, like a ruling committee or oligarchy (Daniel 7:7,24). These ten leaders are pictured as ten toes on the image in Daniel 2 and ten horns on a beast in Daniel 7. I like to call this the Group of Ten or G-10. Later, this group will give its authority to one man, known as the little horn in Daniel 7:8. He will consolidate power in the area of the historical Roman Empire, probably including North Africa and Western Asia as well as the core of his empire in Europe. In the final phase of this end-time Roman Empire, this Western leader, known in the New Testament as the Antichrist or Beast, will extend his rule to the entire world. His global kingdom will last for the final half (three-and-a-half years) of what the Bible calls the time of "Tribulation." He and his kingdom will be suddenly and completely destroyed by the Lord Jesus Christ at His coming.

This second signpost is not fully in place yet since the reunited Roman Empire is not ruled over by ten leaders. Yet we can watch current developments in Europe with great interest. The Bible predicts that when these ten leaders and the nations they represent come together, it won't be easy. It will be like trying to mix iron and clay (Daniel 2:42-43). This mention of iron and clay, or inherent strength and weakness at the same time, is reflected in the European Union today. The EU has great economic and political clout, but its diversity in culture, language, and politics is also ever-present. It represents the joining of strong nations with weak ones, just as Daniel predicted. This corresponds to what we see developing today. One can easily see how the EU could develop into the feet and toes of iron and clay.

The Road to Peace

The third signpost, as we discussed in chapter 6, is the worldwide cry for peace. As everyone knows, the world today is in the throes of struggle and conflict, primarily centered in the Middle East, with Israel at the vortex. The Bible predicts that a time of peace is coming for Israel and even briefly for the entire world (1 Thessalonians 5:1-3).

The Rise of Globalism

The fourth significant signpost is the dramatic move toward globalization. The end-time prophecy of a one-world government and economy, prophesied in Revelation 13 and 17, looks more and more like a mirror of our modern society. Our world is shrinking fast. Exponential technological advances have torn down walls between governments and economies and have exposed everyone to immediate access to information.

Scripture foresaw this exact situation in Revelation 13, where one man will eventually seize world power, establishing a worldwide kingdom for the first time since the days just after the flood under Nimrod (Genesis 10–11). The sudden, stunning rise of globalism is a sure sign of the times.

The Reduction of America

The United States is strangely absent from the prophetic Scriptures. As we noted in chapter 5, this silence is significant. World power in the end times is concentrated in a powerful Western confederacy headed by the Antichrist. This alliance will eventually dominate the world landscape (Revelation 13:4). Since this is true, America will not be the world leader of the end times. What will happen to America is not known with certainty, but the current slide of American power and influence is paving the way for greater globalism and the rise of other international alliances to power, just as Scripture predicts.

The Rumors of War in the Middle East

The sixth significant sign of the end times is the seemingly endless Middle East crisis. Everyone knows that pressure is building in the Middle East. The lid could blow off at any time. How much longer can the tensions be held in check? Anyone who follows the news, even casually, knows that the Middle East is engulfed in the fires of revolution. Egypt has been taken over by the

Muslim Brotherhood. Syria is descending into chaos, and radicals could easily assume the reins of power and take control of Syria's sizable military assets. Iran has threatened to wipe Israel off the map and is rattling the sabers of war. The clouds of war are gathering. The Middle East is ready to go off and the only answer is a comprehensive peace treaty like the one predicted in Scripture.

PUTTING THE PIECES TOGETHER

Never before in human history has there been such a convergence of trends and developments that are part of the matrix of end-time events predicted in Scripture. The major actors are already in the wings waiting for their moment on center stage. The necessary props are moving into place. The prophetic play could begin any moment. The Middle East dominates the attention of the world. Domino revolutions are spreading, and the Middle East is burning. With the eruption of the "Arab Spring," the entire landscape of the Middle East changed in a matter of days and weeks, and in the ensuing months, it continues to morph before our eyes. The Jewish people are regathering and surviving. The Russian bear is dramatically emerging from its brief hibernation. Iran is rising and closing in on its nuclear goal. Europe, although currently struggling, is uniting. The United States is declining economically and politically, paving the way for the rise of greater globalism. The world is clamoring for peace. And world events have never before had such an immediate, instantaneous impact. Decades ago, some events would have taken months or even years to bring about change. But now, these same kinds of events take minutes. The stunning pace of change and the incredible acceleration of impact and effect create a sense in all of us that we are moving toward a great crisis. Events are happening so quickly that it's difficult to keep up.

So far in this book, we have considered a few of the events the Bible predicts for the future of the Middle East and the world, and we have attempted to relate current events to what the Scriptures prophesy. At this point, I want to try to bring it all together—to bring these events into tight focus.

From my study of Bible prophecy, here's my best effort at this time to put the pieces together. Here's a sequence of ten key events that I see looming on the horizon.

1. World tensions will continue to build. The world will continue to turn against Israel as she struggles for survival in a sea of enemies. Israel, Islam, terror, the threat of nuclear jihad, rolling Middle East revolutions, and oil will dominate world news, riveting world focus on the Middle East. The Israel-Iran crisis will eventually erupt into war, possibly escalating into a regional war. Worldwide recession may ensue. The worldwide cry for peace, security, and stability will reach a deafening crescendo.

2. Someday, without any warning, Jesus will come to take His bride to heaven. All believers in Christ will be whisked away to the Father's house in heaven. All unbelievers will be left behind. This event, known as the rapture, will come without any warning. Other events *may* precede it, but no events *must* precede it. It can happen at any moment. It's not necessarily immediate—happening in the next moment—but it is imminent. It could happen at any moment. The rapture will serve as the prophetic trigger that will unleash a series of events predicted in Scripture for the end times.

3. The United States will be greatly affected by the rapture, losing millions of its citizens. In the wake of the rapture and its devastating results on the U.S. economy, world power will shift dramatically away from the U.S. to Europe and Asia.

4. Out of the chaos and confusion created by the rapture, the Antichrist will rise from a reunited form of the Roman Empire led by an oligarchy or ruling committee consisting of ten leaders. This revived or reunited Roman Empire will probably be some future form of what today is called the European Union. This final Roman prince will make a seven-year peace treaty with Israel, ushering in a brief season of

worldwide peace (Ezekiel 38:8,11; Daniel 9:27; 1 Thessalonians 5:1-2; Revelation 6:1-2). The world will enter into a kind of new *Pax Romana* (Roman Peace).

5. In brokering the Middle East peace deal, the Antichrist will temporarily end the threat of terror and instability and guarantee the uninterrupted flow of oil to the West. He will be hailed as a great peacemaker. At last, it will appear that the world has what it has waited for—peace and prosperity.

6. The world's utopia won't last long. Sometime during the first half of the Tribulation, the coalition of nations in Ezekiel 38 will stage a surprise attack on Israel when she has let down her guard. Russia's expanding power, influence, and alliances in the Middle East will be the hooks in the jaws that will drag her reluctantly into this course of action. The attack will be against both Israel and the West, since Israel will be joined to the Antichrist by her treaty. By this invasion of Israel, Russia, Iran, Turkey, Libya, Sudan, the nations of Central Asia, Egypt, and possibly other nations will hope to draw the West into open confrontation—or a final great clash of civilizations.

7. God will supernaturally intervene, just like in Old Testament times, to miraculously rescue

Israel from total annihilation and destroy the invaders.

8. The power vacuum created by the destruction of the armies of Russia, Iran, and most of the other Islamic nations will be quickly filled by the Antichrist. He will seize this opportunity to invade Israel, breaking his covenant. Then, he will move against the helpless nations of Egypt, Libya, and Sudan as he launches his world empire at the midpoint of the seven-year Tribulation. He will establish a headquarters in Babylon (modern Iraq) and seize control of the great oil supply in the Persian Gulf.

9. The Great Tribulation Jesus spoke of in Matthew 24:21 will break out, plunging the world into its final days of darkness and dismay.

10. The world will be saved from the brink of destruction by the Second Coming of Jesus Christ, who will establish His 1000-year kingdom of peace and righteousness on the earth.

In a book I helped update, titled *Armageddon, Oil, and Terror*, John Walvoord and I included this "Prophetic Checklist for the Nations." I thought it might be helpful to include it here.

A Prophetic Checklist for the Nations

The prophetic events related to the nations can be compiled chronologically. Consider how the following list of significant world events—past, present, and future—shows that the world is being dramatically prepared for end-time events.

1. The establishment of the United Nations began a serious first step toward world government.

2. The rebuilding of Europe after World War II made a revival of the Roman Empire possible.

3. Israel was reestablished as a nation.

4. Russia rose to world power and became the ally of the Islamic world.

5. The Common Market and World Bank showed the need for some international regulation of the world economy.

6. China rose to world power and developed the capacity to field a massive army.

7. The Middle East became the most significant trouble spot in the world.

8. The oil blackmail awakened the world to the new concentration of wealth and power in the Middle East.

9. The Iron Curtain fell, removing the final barrier to the revival of the Roman Empire.

10. The world clamors for peace because of the continued disruption caused by the high price of oil, terrorist incidents, and the confused military situation in the Middle East.

11. Ten leaders (the "Group of Ten") will emerge from a European and Mediterranean Coalition—beginnings of the last stage of the prophetic fourth-world empire.

12. In a dramatic power play, a new Mediterranean leader will uproot three leaders of the coalition and take control of the powerful ten-leader group.

13. The new Mediterranean leader will negotiate a "final" peace settlement in the Middle East (broken three-and-a-half years later).

14. Russia and her Islamic allies will attempt an invasion of Israel but will be miraculously destroyed.

15. The Mediterranean leader will proclaim himself world dictator, break his peace settlement with Israel, and declare himself to be God.

16. The new world dictator will desecrate the temple in Jerusalem.

17. The terrible judgments of the great Tribulation will be poured out on the nations of the world.

18. Worldwide rebellion will threaten the world dictator's rule as armies from throughout the world converge on the Middle East for World War III.

19. Christ will return to earth with His armies from heaven.

20. The armies of the world will unite to resist Christ's coming and will be destroyed in the Battle of Armageddon.

21. Christ will establish His millennial reign on earth, ending the times of the Gentiles.

You have to admit—that's quite a forecast. The earth appears to be on the verge of entering into its most dangerous and difficult days. We all need to be praying regularly for Israel and the people of the Middle East. The people there are in the grip of false religion and brutal dictators who oppress and take advantage of them. This is all the more reason the church must seek to reach all of the Middle East and North Africa with the gospel of Jesus Christ before it is too late. Please be praying faithfully for the dear people in these nations at this critical hour.

Another critical thing that each of us need to do is pause and consider where we stand personally with the

Lord. Nothing we can do is more important. The Middle East faces a crisis that could easily erupt into a regional war or something even worse. Certainly the already wobbly world economy will take a major hit. People everywhere will be affected.

Times are uncertain, and the prophetic signposts seem to be aligning, just as the Bible predicted. Where will you go when the rapture occurs? Will you be taken or left behind? Or what will happen to you if you die first? This is the question of utmost importance for every person.

CHAPTER NINE

Do Not Let Your Heart Be Troubled

Finding Peace in a World at War

"Do not let your heart be troubled; believe in God, believe also in Me. In My Father's house are many dwelling places; if it were not so, I would have told you; for I go to prepare a place for you. If I go and prepare a place for you, I will come again and receive you to Myself, that where I am, there you may be also."

Jesus Christ (John 14:1-3)

Years ago, the noted English agnostic Thomas Huxley was in Dublin, Ireland, for some speaking engagements. On one occasion, he left his hotel in a hurry to catch a train, taking one of the city's famous horse-drawn taxis. Huxley thought that the doorman at the hotel had told the driver where he was going, so he simply settled

back in the cab and told the man at the reins to drive
fast. The driver set off at a furious pace. In a few minutes,
Huxley realized that the cab was headed away from the
station. "Do you know where you're going?" he shouted
to the driver. "No, your honor," the driver answered, "but
I'm driving fast."

This story sums up the spirit of our own tumultuous,
troubled times. There is furious motion, great speed, yet
few seem to know where they are or where they're headed.
For our modern world, life is like Franklin Delano Roosevelt described it in his first inaugural address: "We don't
know where we are going but we are on our way."[1] That's
an apt picture of our world today.

But as we've seen, we can know where we're going. We
don't know everything that's coming, but we can see that
the specific signposts that point to the end times are lining up. The stage is being set for the opening act of the
most astonishing drama of history. As we watch the Middle East simmer, boil, and explode, it appears that the
curtain could go up at any time and the drama could
begin.

What should our response be to all of this? Should we
fold in fear? Or wither in worry?

It's critical for us to remember that God did not give
us Bible prophecy to *scare* us but to *prepare* us. He didn't
give it to us to make us *anxious*, but to make us *aware*. So,
how should we prepare for what's coming? How should
you respond? Your response depends on where you stand
with the Lord.

What Prophecy Means to the Unbeliever

A Scottish surgeon named Sir James Simpson was one of Queen Victoria's trusted royal physicians. The Scottish people loved Dr. Simpson deeply. In honor of this godly man, 80,000 Scots watched his funeral procession in Edinburgh.

In 1847, Dr. Simpson made an important discovery. While conducting experiments with chloroform, he realized that by using chloroform, doctors could perform operations without causing pain to their patients. His discovery revolutionized modern medicine. Toward the end of his life, Simpson was lecturing at the University of Edinburgh. One of the students asked him what he considered his most valuable discovery. The students expected him to recount how he came upon the medical use of chloroform. To the surprise of the students, Dr. Simpson replied, "My most valuable discovery was when I discovered myself a sinner and that Jesus Christ was my Savior."[2] Not long after those words, when he was dying in extreme pain, he commented, "When I think, it is of the words 'Jesus only,' and really, that is all that is needed, is it not?"

Have you made life's greatest discovery? Have you discovered that you are a sinner and that Jesus Christ is your Savior? Have you found that "Jesus only" is all that you need for salvation from your sins? If not, why not trust Him now?

No person knows how much time he has left on this earth, either personally or prophetically. Personally, all of

us are painfully aware of our mortality. We have no guarantee we will see tomorrow. Prophetically, Christ could
come at any moment to take His bride, the church, to
heaven, and all unbelievers will be left behind to endure
the horrors of the Tribulation period.

With this in mind, the most important question for
every reader to face is whether he or she has a personal
relationship with Jesus Christ as Savior. The message of
salvation through Jesus Christ contains both bad news
and good news.

The bad news is that the Bible declares that all people,
including you and me, are sinful and therefore separated
from the Holy God of the universe (Isaiah 59:2; Romans
3:23). God is holy and cannot just overlook sin. A just
payment for the debt must be made. But we are spiritu-
ally bankrupt, and we have no resources within ourselves
to pay the huge debt we owe.

The good news (or gospel) is that Jesus Christ has
come and satisfied our sin debt. He bore our judgment
and paid the price for our sins. He died on the cross for
our sins and was raised to life on the third day to prove
conclusively that the work of salvation had been fully
accomplished. Colossians 2:14 says that He "canceled
out the certificate of debt consisting of decrees against
us, which was hostile to us; and He has taken it out of
the way, having nailed it to the cross." First Peter 3:18
says, "Christ also died for sins once for all, the just for the
unjust, so that He might bring us to God."

The salvation that Christ accomplished for us is

available to all through faith in Jesus Christ. Salvation from sin is a free gift that God offers to sinful people who deserve judgment. Won't you receive the gift today? Place your faith and trust in Christ and in Him alone for your eternal salvation. The Bible makes it crystal clear:

- "Believe in the Lord Jesus, and you will be saved" (Acts 16:31).

- "But as many as received Him, to them He gave the right to become children of God, even to those who believe in His name" (John 1:12).

Now that you know the truth of the rapture and that those who fail to trust Christ will be left behind to endure the terrible Tribulation, won't you respond to the invitation before it is too late?

Accept Christ personally by calling upon Him to save you from your sins. You can do it right now, right where you are. Make sure you're ready when Jesus comes!

What Prophecy Means to the Believer

God spent a great deal of time and ink telling us what to expect in the future. One out of every thirteen verses in the New Testament relate to the coming of Christ. Our Lord's coming is mentioned over 300 times in the 260 chapters of the New Testament. So, clearly, it's important. But while it's key that we hold this truth, it's equally important that this truth hold us. That it makes a practical difference in how we live each day. That it motivates us to live godly lives in the present.

Every key New Testament prophetic passage contains practical application closely associated with it. Prophecy was not given just to stir our imagination or capture our attention. Prophecy is intended by God to change our attitudes and actions to be more in line with His Word and His character.

Prophecy expert Charles Dyer emphasizes this purpose of Bible prophecy:

> God gave prophecy to change our hearts, not to fill our heads with knowledge. God never predicted future events just to satisfy our curiosity about the future. Every time God announces events that are future, He includes with His predictions practical applications to life. God's pronouncements about the future carry with them specific advice for the "here and now."[3]

According to the Bible, there are many life-changing effects or influences that understanding the future is to have on our hearts. Here are five key ones for us to apply to our lives.

We Have Hope and Peace in Troubled Times

I had the privilege of attending the Fiesta Bowl with my family in January 2012 to watch our alma mater, the

Oklahoma State University Cowboys, play the Stanford Cardinal. Oklahoma State fell down early 14-0 but came roaring back. The game was exciting and nerve-racking. Stanford missed a late chip shot field goal to seal the victory, and the game went into overtime. Stanford got the ball first and missed another field goal. With the ball on the one yard line, Oklahoma State kicked a field goal, pulling out the victory in stunning fashion.

When we got back to our room later that night, my sons and I turned on the television, and the channel was replaying the game we had just finished watching a few hours earlier. That's pretty incredible to watch a replay that quickly. We sat down to watch it, and I have to say that I was much more relaxed watching the replay. Even when OSU fell behind on numerous occasions, I was totally relaxed. No sweat. Why? I already knew the outcome. I knew that we won. None of the setbacks, turnovers, or missed opportunities caused me the least bit of anxiety. I knew how it would finally end. I even went to bed before the replay was over.

There's something about knowing the outcome in advance that brings us peace and rest. The same should be true of our lives now. While we don't know every detail of what's ahead, we do know who wins. The final score is already in the Book. Knowing what's ahead gives us hope, comfort, and confidence in a troubled, uncertain world.

Our world is drowning in discouragement and uncertainty. Most people feel as if they've lost control of their destiny. People everywhere today seem more downcast, discouraged, and even more depressed than ever before. News on every front is troubling: Political impotence and irresponsibility exist in our government, economic fear and uncertainty continues, and wars and rumors of wars happen all over the world. Added to these problems are the personal trials and difficulties we all face. Trouble is the common denominator of all mankind. Yet, even in a world where the Niagara of bad news never seems to end, we have hope. We know how the story ends. God has given us glimpses of the future to reassure us that He is in total control.

Someday Jesus will come to take us to be with Himself. Jesus gave this promise in John 14:1-3:

> Do not let your heart be troubled; believe in God, believe also in Me. In My Father's house are many dwelling places; if it were not so, I would have told you; for I go to prepare a place for you. If I go and prepare a place for you, I will come again and receive you to Myself, that where I am, there you may be also.

In these verses, three points are emphasized—a person, a place, and a promise. The person is Jesus, the place is heaven, and the promise is that He will come again someday to take His people there.

We Are Encouraged to Meet Together Regularly and Strengthen One Another

Hebrews 10:24-25 reminds us to "consider how to stimulate one another to love and good deeds, not forsaking our own assembling together, as is the habit of some, but encouraging one another; and all the more as you see the day drawing near." The writer of Hebrews reminds us that as the days get darker and the time of the Lord's coming draws near, we should be prompted more than ever to gather together with God's people for encouragement and strength. Don't get isolated from other believers. We need each other. Far too many professing Christians today are not vitally connected to a local church. You need to allow God to use you to bring encouragement to others in their time of need and let others minister to you when you need to be uplifted. But we can't do this effectively if we are never with one another living out the life-on-life contact God intended in the local church.

Find a local church that believes and teaches God's Word and get involved there using the gifts and abilities God has given you to build up others and glorify God. As we see the day of the Lord's coming drawing near, we are encouraged more and more to support and help one another.

We Can Have an Eternal Perspective in a Shortsighted World

One of the advantages God's people have is a long-term perspective, as 2 Corinthians 4:16-18 reminds us:

> Therefore we do not lose heart, but though our outer man is decaying, yet our inner man is being renewed day by day. For momentary, light affliction is producing for us an eternal weight of glory far beyond all comparison, while we look not at the things which are seen, but at the things which are not seen; for the things which are seen are temporal, but the things which are not seen are eternal.

In a world that's dominated by the 24-hour news cycle of cable TV and up-to-the-minute events, we can see the distant horizon and know where it's all headed. We can see beyond the temporal to the eternal and beyond what's seen to what's unseen.

We Can Live Pure Lives in Evil Days

The world exerts its strong pull on our lives enticing us to live according to its values and mind-set. The Word of God is clear that a proper understanding of Bible prophecy inspires us to lives of holiness and purity. Peter drives this point home:

But the day of the Lord will come like a thief, in which the heavens will pass away with a roar and the elements will be destroyed with intense heat, and the earth and its works will be burned up. Since all these things are to be destroyed in this way, what sort of people ought you to be in holy conduct and godliness, looking for and hastening the coming of the day of God, because of which the heavens will be destroyed by burning, and the elements will melt with intense heat! But according to His promise we are looking for new heavens and a new earth, in which righteousness dwells. Therefore, beloved, since you look for these things, be diligent to be found by Him in peace, spotless and blameless (2 Peter 3:10-14).

Paul also encourages believers, "Live sensibly, righteously and godly in the present age, looking for the blessed hope and the appearing of the glory of our great God and Savior, Jesus Christ" (Titus 2:12-13).

Prophecy and purity are mentioned together in Romans 13:11-14:

This is all the more urgent, for you know how late it is; time is running out. Wake up, for our salvation is nearer now than when we first believed. The night is almost gone; the day of salvation will soon be here. So remove your dark deeds like dirty clothes, and put on the shining

armor of right living. Because we belong to
the day, we must live decent lives for all to see.
Don't participate in the darkness of wild parties and drunkenness, or in sexual promiscuity
and immoral living, or in quarreling and jeal-
ously. But let the Lord Jesus Christ take control
of you, and don't think of ways to indulge your
evil desires (NLT).

One final verse is 1 John 3:2-3: "Beloved, now we are
children of God, and it has not appeared as yet what we
will be. We know that when He appears, we will be like
Him, because we will see Him just as He is. And everyone who has this hope fixed on Him purifies himself, just
as He is pure."

In light of what we know is coming, we should live
our lives in a way that pleases God and reflects our understanding of the ultimate destiny of ourselves and this
world. We should live for what lasts rather than spending
our efforts pursuing empty, earthly pleasures.

WE ARE MOTIVATED TO SHARE GOD'S GOOD NEWS WITH OTHERS

Knowing what's ahead for this world and for those
who are outside of Christ should serve as a supreme stim-
ulus for all who know Him to share the good news with
others. The apostle Paul wrote his final inspired letter,
known as 2 Timothy, from a Roman prison cell. The letter was directed to his co-laborer Timothy. It's clear from

the letter that Paul knew tumultuous times were ahead and that Timothy could be tempted to give up.

One of Paul's final appeals is based on end-time events.

> I solemnly charge you in the presence of God and of Christ Jesus, who is to judge the living and the dead, and by His appearing and His kingdom: preach the word; be ready in season and out of season; reprove, rebuke, exhort, with great patience and instruction…But you, be sober in all things, endure hardship, do the work of an evangelist, fulfill your ministry (2 Timothy 4:1-2,5).

Paul knew that danger was on the horizon, but he looked far beyond the impending trouble to the time of Christ's coming and the final judgment. In light of that day, Paul urged Timothy and each of us to faithfully proclaim the good news as an evangelist (one who brings good news). All who know Christ should do all we can to give as many people as possible the opportunity to hear the good news of forgiveness and eternal life through faith in Jesus.

We are Christ's ambassadors in a foreign land. It's up to us as God's people to spread the good news of salvation through Jesus Christ. "Therefore, we are ambassadors for Christ, as though God were making an appeal through us; we beg you on behalf of Christ, be reconciled to God" (2 Corinthians 5:20).

God's message of what's coming is not only to fill our heads but also to change our hearts. When the events outlined in this book are fulfilled (and they may be very soon), what difference should it make in your life today? The answer to that question could well decide your eternal destiny.

The Persia Prophecies

W inston Churchill once said, "The farther backward you can look, the farther forward you are likely to see." The same is true when it comes to understanding Bible prophecy. The past fulfillment of prophecy establishes the pattern for future fulfillment. With this maxim in mind, let's survey what Scripture says about Persia (Iran) in the past and how that affects what we see today.

The words *Persia*, *Persian*, and *Persians* occur a total of 35 times in the Old Testament. Thirty-four of these references clearly refer to the ancient Persian Empire and have, therefore, already been literally fulfilled. However, the reference to Persia in Ezekiel 38:5 is still future in our day and refers to the modern nation of Iran. The name was changed from Persia to Iran in 1935 and then to the Islamic Republic of Iran in 1979.

This book is primarily about current events in the Middle East and future prophecies of Iran and Israel. But many may not be aware that the Bible has accurately prophesied events about Israel and Iran (ancient Persia) that have already been fulfilled. Since at least two biblical prophecies about ancient Persia have been literally fulfilled, we can rest assured that when the time comes, the prophecy in Ezekiel 38 will be literally fulfilled as well.

THE CYRUS PROPHECY

The first specific Old Testament prophecy about Persia is found in the writing of the Hebrew prophet Isaiah, who wrote during the Golden Age of the Hebrew prophets in the eighth century BC. His prophecies are astounding in their detail. Writing in about 700 BC, he named the Medo-Persian King "Cyrus" by name about 100 years before he was born and almost 150 years before he rose to power.

Cyrus is a towering figure in Persian history. He led the ancient nation to great victories, territorial expansion, and astounding prosperity. Cyrus began his conquests in about 550 BC, enjoying unparalleled success, but his career culminated when he took the city of Babylon in October 539 BC as recorded in Daniel 5. Isaiah calls him by name and chronicles his reign in detail:

> "It is I who says of Cyrus, 'He is My shepherd! And he will perform all My desire.' And he

declares of Jerusalem, 'She will be built,' and
of the temple, 'Your foundation will be laid.'"
Thus says the LORD to Cyrus, His anointed,
whom I have taken by the right hand to sub-
due nations before him and to loose the loins
of kings; to open doors before him so that gates
will not be shut (Isaiah 44:28–45:1).

If one accepts Isaiah's authorship of the book of Isaiah,
as I do, then there is no other way to understand these
words. Isaiah named King Cyrus about 100 years before
he was born. This sets the Bible apart from any other
book that's ever been written.

Isaiah 41:2-4 and verse 25 clearly make reference to
Cyrus, but Isaiah 44:28 and 45:1 specifically name him.
Isaiah 45:2-6 goes on to predict the conquests of Cyrus
and his restoration of the Jewish people to their land. Isaiah 44:28 specifically foretells his restoration of the Jews
to their land and their temple worship: "It is I who says of
Cyrus, 'He is my shepherd! And he will perform all My
desire.' And he declares of Jerusalem, 'She will be built,'
and of the temple, 'Your foundation will be laid.'" This
was dramatically fulfilled in 2 Chronicles 36:22-23:

Now in the first year of Cyrus king of Persia—
in order to fulfill the word of the LORD by the
mouth of Jeremiah—the LORD stirred up the
spirit of Cyrus king of Persia, so that he sent a
proclamation throughout all his kingdom, and

also put it in writing, saying, "Thus says Cyrus
king of Persia, 'The LORD, the God of heaven,
has given me all the kingdoms of the earth, and
He has appointed me to build Him a house in
Jerusalem, which is in Judah. Whoever there is
among you of all His people, may the LORD his
God be with him, and let him go up!'" (see also
Ezra 1:1-11).

Liberal critics who deny the inspiration of the Bible
and approach it with an anti-supernatual bias reject
any possibility of God foretelling the future. They con-
tend that Isaiah was not written in the eighth century
BC before Cyrus came to power but by someone else
later after Cyrus was already born and accomplished his
exploits.[1] Alfred Martin, an Old Testament scholar, gets
to the heart of the issue:

This is actually the crux of the problem as far as
the attitude of critics toward the Book of Isaiah is concerned…Here is Isaiah in the eighth
century B.C. announcing Cyrus as the restorer
of the people to Jerusalem, Cyrus who lived in
the sixth century B.C.…. The whole point of the
passage is that God, the omniscient God, is the
One who announces events beforehand. That
is the proof of His deity. The destructive critics
who say this passage must have been written in
the sixth century by some otherwise unknown

prophet in the Babylon ("Deutero-Isaiah") are making the same stupid mistake that the idolaters of Isaiah's day were making. They are like the Sadducees of another time, to whom the Lord Jesus Christ said, "Ye do err, not knowing the scriptures, nor the power of God" (Matt. 22:39).[2]

It's incredible that critics who deny the authenticity of Isaiah totally miss the point. The Cyrus prophecies are found in Isaiah 41–45, a section of the Bible that is extolling God as the only One who can accurately foretell the future. The Cyrus prophecies are set forth by God as "Exhibit A" of His ability to predict events before they occur. Notice how many times in the surrounding context of Isaiah that God drives home this point that only He can accurately forecast the future.

Isaiah 41:21-24

"Present your case," the LORD says. "Bring forward your strong arguments," the king of Jacob says. Let them bring forth and declare to us what is going to take place; as the former events, declare what they were, that we may consider them and know their outcome. Or announce to us what is coming; declare the things that are going to come afterward, that we may know that you are gods; indeed, do good or evil, that we may anxiously look about us and fear together. Behold, you are of no account, and your work amounts to nothing; he who chooses you is an abomination.

Isaiah 42:9

Behold, the former things have come to pass, now I declare new things; before they spring forth I proclaim them to you.

Isaiah 45:21

Declare and set forth your case; indeed, let them consult together. Who has announced this from of old? Who has long since declared it? Is it not I, the LORD? And there is no other God besides Me, a righteous God and a Savior; there is none except Me.

Isaiah 46:9-10

> Remember the former things long past, for I
> am God, and there is no other; I am God, and
> there is no one like Me, declaring the end from
> the beginning, and from ancient times things
> which have not been done, saying, "My purpose
> will be established, and I will accomplish all my
> good pleasure."

The very next words after Isaiah 46:9-10, where God proclaims that only He can tell the future, are a direct prophecy about Cyrus the Great: "Calling a bird of prey from the east, the man of My purpose from a far country. Truly I have spoken; truly I will bring it to pass. I have planned it, surely I will do it" (Isaiah 46:11).

God likens Cyrus to a bird of prey that He will summon from the east to accomplish His purposes.

Liberal critics would strip away the key prophecy in this section that God provides to prove that He is the only true God as He repeatedly affirms in Isaiah 41–46. Adopting their view would mean that God is no different from idols—the very point that Isaiah is disproving. Nevertheless, despite their unbelief, the Cyrus prophecy stands firm as the ultimate proof of the truth of these amazing claims and serves as the first great Old Testament prophecy about Persia.

DANIEL AND THE LATTER DAYS

The other main Old Testament predictions about Persia are found in the prophecies of Daniel. Three times Daniel predicted the rise of Persia on the heels of the Babylonian Empire.

Daniel 2: The Silver Kingdom

Daniel 2 records the dream of the Babylonian king Nebuchadnezzar and the interpretation of that dream by Daniel. In his dream Nebuchadnezzar saw a huge statue of man consisting of four different materials. The four metals in the great statue represented four great empires that would appear successively on the world scene to rule over the civilized world of that day and on into the end times. With 20/20 hindsight of history, we now know that these four empires were Babylon, Medo-Persia, Greece, and Rome. The feet and the ten toes of iron and clay point forward, even from our day, to a final, ten-king form of the Roman Empire. Daniel predicted the rise of the Persian Empire while Babylon was still ruling and accurately saw the future fall of Persia to Greece, which occurred two hundred years after Daniel died. The transfer of power from Babylon to Persia occurred on October 12, 539 BC, and is recorded in dramatic fashion in Daniel 5.

Daniel 7: The Big Bear

Daniel 7 covers the same material in Daniel 2, yet with different imagery. Here the four empires are pictured not as metals but as monsters.

In the first year of Belshazzar king of Babylon Daniel saw a dream and visions in his mind as he lay on his bed; then he wrote the dream down and related the following summary of it. Daniel said, "I was looking in my vision by night, and behold, the four winds of heaven were stirring up the great sea. And four great beasts were coming up from the sea, different from one another. The first was like a lion and had the wings of an eagle. I kept looking until its wings were plucked, and it was lifted up from the ground and made to stand on two feet like a man; a human mind also was given to it. And behold, another beast, a second one, resembling a bear. And it was raised up on one side, and three ribs were in its mouth between its teeth; and thus they said to it, 'Arise, devour much meat!' After this I kept looking, and behold, another one, like a leopard, which had on its back four wings of a bird; the beast also had four heads, and dominion was given to it" (Daniel 7:1-6).

Babylon, the winged lion, is replaced by Persia, the bloodthirsty bear which in turn is conquered by the Greek empire, pictured as a four-headed leopard with four wings. All this happened in history just as the Bible predicted.

Daniel 8: East Meets West

The final main Persian prophecy from Daniel was given in chapter 8 where the Persian Empire was pictured as a mighty two-horned ram that is gored and killed by a powerful goat with a large horn that symbolized the Greek Empire led by Alexander the Great. The imagery is confirmed in Daniel 8:20-21: "The ram which you saw with the two horns represents the kings of Media and Persia. And the shaggy goat represents the kingdom of Greece: and the large horn that is between his eyes is the first king." East met west, and the west won.

History in Advance

The ancient Persian Empire ruled the world for two hundred years (539–331 BC) in power and human splendor as the silver kingdom, the bloodthirsty bear, and the two-horned ram just as Daniel predicted. But, in 331 BC, her splendor was ruined by the Greek Empire, which is represented by the bronze kingdom in Daniel 2, the four-headed leopard in Daniel 7, and the male goat in Daniel 8. The prophecies of Scripture concerning Persia were all fulfilled to a tee.

After Persia's demise in the fourth century BC, she passed off the scene as a major power and eventually deteriorated into a second-rate nation with little power or prestige in the world. However, in the last 35 years, that situation has been dramatically reversed. Today, Iran is the major player in the Middle East. The rise of Iran is a key stage-setting event for the events of the end times. Iran must become a key player in the Middle East

for the ancient prophecy of Ezekiel 38–39 to be fulfilled. The final prophecies of Iran in Ezekiel 38–39 will
be fulfilled just as literally and specifically as the ones
that have already come to pass given to us by Isaiah and
Daniel.

America in Prophecy
(Dr. John F. Walvoord)

In our current age, we often fail to keep in touch with the past. Great teachers are too quickly forgotten. One of my teachers was Dr. John F. Walvoord, who served as president of Dallas Theological Seminary for 35 years. I've included this excerpt from his 1967 work *The Nations in Prophecy* so you can learn from his wise words, which still ring true today:

"AMERICA IN PROPHECY," BY DR. JOHN F. WALVOORD

One of the natural questions facing the world, but especially citizens of the United States of America, is the place of the United States in the unfulfilled prophetic program. In the last 50 years, the United States of America has become one of the most powerful and influential nations of all history. What does the Bible contribute to the question of the future of the United States?

In keeping with the principle that prophecy is primarily concerned with the Holy Land and its immediate neighbors, it is not surprising that geographic areas remote from this center of biblical interest should not figure largely in prophecy and may not be mentioned at all. No specific mention of the United States or any other country in North or South America can be found in the Bible. None of the rather obscure references to distant lands can be taken specifically as a reference to the United States. Any final answer to the question is therefore an impossibility, but nevertheless some conclusions of a general character can be reached.

The World Situation in the End Times

As previous study of prophecy has indicated, the Scriptures provide an outline of major events in the period beginning with the rapture of the church and ending with the second coming of Christ to establish His kingdom. Immediately after the rapture, there will be a period of preparation in which the ten-nation confederacy in the Mediterranean will emerge and the little horn of Daniel 7 will be revealed as its eventual dictator. At the same time, there will be the emergence of a world church as suggested in Revelation 17.

At the conclusion of this period of preparation, the head of the Mediterranean confederacy, who will be the Roman "prince that shall come," will make a covenant with Israel (Daniel 9:27), which will introduce the second phase of the period, namely, a period of protection and peace for Israel. After enduring for three-and-a-half years or one-half of the projected seven-year period contemplated in the covenant, the Roman ruler will take the role of world dictator, assume the prerogatives of deity, and begin the great Tribulation with its corresponding period of persecution for Israel and the emergence of a world religion with the world ruler as its deity. This third period will be climaxed by the second coming of Christ to the earth and its attending judgments.

The Relation of the United States to These World Events

Although the Scriptures do not give any clear word concerning the role of the United States in relationship to the revived Roman Empire and the later development of the world empire, it is probable that the United States will be in some form of alliance with the Roman ruler. Most citizens of the United States of America have come from Europe and their sympathies would be more naturally with a European alliance than with Russia or countries in Eastern Asia. It may even be that the United States will provide large support for the Mediterranean confederacy, as it seems to be in opposition to Russia, Eastern Asia, and Africa. Actually, a balance of power in the world may exist at that time not too dissimilar to the present world situation—namely, that Europe and the Mediterranean area will be in alliance with America in opposition to Russia, Eastern Asia, and Africa. Based on geographic, religious, and economic factors such an alliance of powers seems a natural sequence of present situations in the world.

If the end-time events include a destruction of Russia and her allies prior to the final period of the great Tribulation, this may trigger an unbalance in the world situation that will permit the Roman ruler to become a world ruler. In this event, it should be clear that the United States will be in a subordinate role and no longer the great international power that it is today.

It has been suggested by some that the total absence of Scriptural comment on the United States of America in the end times is evidence that the United States previously has been destroyed by an atomic war or some other catastrophic means and therefore no longer is a voice in international affairs. Such a solution, however, overlooks the fact that not only the United States but all of the Americas are omitted from prophecy, and the same is true of Australia. The fact is there are few references to any country at some distance from the Holy Land. The view, therefore, would be preferable that while the United States is in existence and possibly a power to be reckoned with in the rapidly moving events that characterize the end of the age, world political power will be centered in the Mediterranean area, and necessarily the United States will play a subordinate role.

History has many records of great nations that have risen to unusual power and influence, only to decline because of internal corruption or international complications. It may well be that the United States of America is today at the zenith of its power much as Babylon was in the sixth century BC prior to its sudden downfall at the hands of the Medes and the Persians (Daniel 5). Any realistic survey of moral conditions in the world today would justify a judgment of God on any nation, including that of the United States. The longsuffering God has offered unusual benefits to the United States, both in a material and religious way, but they have been used with such profligacy that ultimate divine judgment may be expected. The question no longer is whether America deserves judgment, but rather why divine judgment has been so long withheld from a nation which has enjoyed so much of God's bounty.

A partial answer may be found in the fact that the United States of America in spite of its failures has nevertheless been a source of major Christian testimony in the world and has done more to promote the missionary cause in terms of money and men than any other nation. Although the United States numbers only five per cent of the total world population, in the last century probably more than fifty per cent of the missionaries and money spent has come from America. In view of the fact that it is God's major purpose in this present age to call out Jew and Gentile to faith in Christ and to have the Gospel preached in all nations, the prosperity which has been true of America has made possible this end and may have been permitted by God to accomplish His holy purposes.

Another important reason for delay in divine judgment upon America is the Abrahamic promise concerning his seed, "I will bless them that bless thee, and curse him that curseth thee" (Genesis 12:3). The United States for the most part has been kind to the Jew. Here the seed of Abraham has had religious freedom and opportunity to make wealth. Judgment on other nations has frequently been preceded by persecution of the Jew. So far in the United States the Jew has had equal treatment.

It is evident, however, that if Christ came for His church and all true Christians were caught out of this world, America then would be reduced to the same situation as other countries. The true church will be gone, and Israel may be persecuted. The drastically changed situation would no longer call for material or political blessing upon the United States. It would therefore follow that with the removal of the principal cause for withholding judgment, namely, the promotion of the missionary cause and befriending the wandering Jew, reason would no longer exist for maintaining America in its present standard of power politically and economically. It may well be that the United States, like Babylon of old, will lose its place of leadership in the world, and this will be a major cause in the shift of power to the Mediterranean scene.

Conclusion

Although conclusions concerning the role of America in prophecy in the end time are necessarily tentative, the Scriptural evidence is sufficient to conclude that America in that day will not be a major power and apparently does not figure largely in either the political, economic, or religious aspects of the world. America may well be at its zenith today both in power, influence, and opportunity.

In view of the imminent return of the Lord, the time is short and the cause of evangelism is urgent. If prophecy has any one message as bearing on our times, it is that time and opportunity are short, and impending world conditions soon may close the door for further witness in many areas. What is true of America is true for the evangelical church throughout the world, and prophecy in general serves to emphasize the importance of the present task of bearing witness to the Gospel, beginning at Jerusalem and to the uttermost parts of the world.

The destiny of nations is in the hands of the omnipotent God. History is moving inexorably to its prophesied consummation. The divine program in all its detail will be fulfilled. The Son of God will reign in Zion. The nations will bow at His feet. Ultimately the present earth will be replaced with a new heaven and a new earth in which the New Jerusalem will be the home of the redeemed of all ages. All nations will continue throughout eternity to worship and adore the infinite Triune God whose majesty, wisdom, and power will be unquestioned. In that eternal day, God's love and grace will be supremely revealed in those among all nations who are redeemed by the blood of the Lamb.

Ezekiel 38–39

Ezekiel 38: And the word of the Lord came to me saying, "Son of man, set your face toward Gog of the land of Magog, the prince of Rosh, Meshech and Tubal, and prophesy against him and say, 'Thus says the Lord God, "Behold, I am against you, O Gog, prince of Rosh, Meshech and Tubal. I will turn you about and put hooks into your jaws, and I will bring you out, and all your army, horses and horsemen, all of them splendidly attired, a great company *with* buckler and shield, all of them wielding swords; Persia, Ethiopia and Put with them, all of them *with* shield and helmet; Gomer with all its troops; Beth-togarmah *from* the remote parts of the north with all its troops—many peoples with you.

"Be prepared, and prepare yourself, you and all your companies that are assembled about you, and be a guard for them. After many days you will be summoned; in the latter years you will come into the land that is restored from the sword, *whose inhabitants* have been gathered from many nations to the mountains of Israel which had been a continual waste; but its people were brought out from the nations, and they are living securely, all of them. You will go up, you will come like a storm; you will be like a cloud covering the land, you and all your troops, and many peoples with you."

'Thus says the Lord GOD, "It will come about on that day, that thoughts will come into your mind and you will devise an evil plan, and you will say, 'I will go up against the land of unwalled villages. I will go against those who are at rest, that live securely, all of them living without walls and having no bars or gates, to capture spoil and to seize plunder, to turn your hand against the waste places which are *now* inhabited, and against the people who are gathered from the nations, who have acquired cattle and goods, who live at the center of the world.' Sheba and Dedan and the merchants of Tarshish with all its villages will say to you, 'Have you come to capture spoil? Have you assembled your company to seize plunder, to carry away silver and gold, to take away cattle and goods, to capture great spoil?'"'

"Therefore prophesy, son of man, and say to Gog, 'Thus says the Lord GOD, "On that day when My people Israel are living securely, will you not know *it*? You will come from your place out of the remote parts of the north, you and many peoples with you, all of them riding on horses, a great assembly and a mighty army; and you will come up against My people Israel like a cloud to cover the land. It shall come about in the last days that I will bring you against My land, so that the nations may know Me when I am sanctified through you before their eyes, O Gog."

'Thus says the Lord GOD, "Are you the one of whom I spoke in former days through My servants the prophets of Israel, who prophesied in those days for *many* years that I would bring you against them? It will come about on that day, when Gog comes against the land of Israel," declares the Lord GOD, "that My fury will mount up in My anger. In My zeal and in My blazing wrath I declare *that* on that day there will surely be a great earthquake in the land of Israel. The fish of the sea, the birds of the heavens, the beasts of the field, all the creeping things that creep on the earth, and all the men who are on the face of the earth will shake at My presence; the mountains also will be thrown down, the steep pathways will collapse and every wall will fall to the ground. I will call for a sword against him on all My mountains," declares the Lord GOD.

"Every man's sword will be against his brother. With pestilence and with blood I will enter into judgment with him; and I will rain on him and on his troops, and on the many peoples who are with him, a torrential rain, with hailstones, fire and brimstone. I will magnify Myself, sanctify Myself, and make Myself known in the sight of many nations; and they will know that I am the LORD."'

EZEKIEL 39: "And you, son of man, prophesy against Gog and say, 'Thus says the Lord GOD, "Behold, I am against you, O Gog, prince of Rosh, Meshech and Tubal; and I will turn you around, drive you on, take you up from the remotest parts of the north and bring you against the mountains of Israel. I will strike your bow from your left hand and dash down your arrows from your right hand. You will fall on the mountains of Israel, you and all your troops and the peoples who are with you; I will give you as food to every kind of predatory bird and beast of the field. You will fall on the open field; for it is I who have spoken," declares the Lord GOD. "And I will send fire upon Magog and those who inhabit the coastlands in safety; and they will know that I am the LORD.

"My holy name I will make known in the midst of My people Israel; and I will not let My holy name be profaned anymore. And the nations will know that I am the LORD, the Holy One in Israel. Behold, it is coming and it shall be done," declares the Lord GOD. "That is the day of which I have spoken.

"Then those who inhabit the cities of Israel will go out and make fires with the weapons and burn *them*, both shields and bucklers, bows and arrows, war clubs and spears, and for seven years they will make fires of them. They will not take wood from the field or gather firewood from the forests, for they will make fires with the weapons; and they will take the spoil of those who despoiled them and seize the plunder of those who plundered them," declares the Lord GOD.

"On that day I will give Gog a burial ground there in Israel, the valley of those who pass by east of the sea, and it will block off those who would pass by. So they will bury Gog there with all his horde, and they will call *it* the valley of Hamon-gog. For seven months the house of Israel will be burying them in order to cleanse the land. Even all the people of the land will bury *them*; and it will be to their renown *on* the day that I glorify Myself," declares the Lord GOD. "They will set apart men who will constantly pass through the land, burying those who were passing through, even those left on the surface of the ground, in order to cleanse it. At the end of seven months they will make a search. As those who pass through the land pass through and anyone sees a man's bone, then he will set up a marker by it until the buriers have buried it in the valley of Hamon-gog. And even *the* name of *the* city will be Hamonah. So they will cleanse the land."'

"As for you, son of man, thus says the Lord GOD, 'Speak to every kind of bird and to every beast of the field, "Assemble and come, gather from every side to My sacrifice which I am going to sacrifice for you, as a great sacrifice on the mountains of Israel, that you may eat flesh and drink blood. You will eat the flesh of mighty men and drink the blood of the princes of the earth, as *though they were* rams, lambs, goats and bulls, all of them fatlings of Bashan. So you will eat fat until you are glutted, and drink blood until you are drunk, from My sacrifice which I have sacrificed for you. You will be glutted at My table with horses and charioteers, with mighty men and all the men of war," declares the Lord GOD.

"And I will set My glory among the nations; and all the nations will see My judgment which I have executed

and My hand which I have laid on them. And the house
of Israel will know that I am the Lord their God from
that day onward. The nations will know that the house of
Israel went into exile for their iniquity because they acted
treacherously against Me, and I hid My face from them;
so I gave them into the hand of their adversaries, and all
of them fell by the sword. According to their unclean-
ness and according to their transgressions I dealt with
them, and I hid My face from them.""""

Therefore thus says the Lord God, "Now I will restore
the fortunes of Jacob and have mercy on the whole house
of Israel; and I will be jealous for My holy name. They
will forget their disgrace and all their treachery which
they perpetrated against Me, when they live securely on
their *own* land with no one to make *them* afraid. When
I bring them back from the peoples and gather them
from the lands of their enemies, then I shall be sanctified through them in the sight of the many nations. Then
they will know that I am the Lord their God because
I made them go into exile among the nations, and then
gathered them *again* to their own land; and I will leave
none of them there any longer. I will not hide My face
from them any longer, for I will have poured out My
Spirit on the house of Israel," declares the Lord God.

Notes

Opening Book Epigraphs

1. Benjamin Netanyahu, speech to American Israel Public Affairs Committee (AIPAC), March 5, 2012.

2. Ehud Barak, as quoted in Dan Williams, "Iran could seek short build time for bomb: Israel," *Reuters*, May 4, 2012, http://msnbc.msn.com/id/47291617, accessed July 26, 2012.

3. Niall Ferguson, "Israel's Case for War with Iran," *Newsweek*, February 13, 2012, 24.

Chapter 1: As Time Runs Out

1. Peter Hirschberg, "Netanhayu: It's 1938 and Iran is Germany," *Haaretz*, November 14, 2006.

2. Gary Sick, CNN.com "What if Israel Bombs Iran," March 30, 2012, www.cnn.com/2012/03/30/opinion/sick-israel-iran/index.html, accessed July 26, 2012.

3. Yaakov Katz and Yoaz Hendel, *Israel vs. Iran: The Shadow War* (Washington, DC: Potomac Books, 2012), 167-68.

4. Matthew Gutman, "Israeli pilot recalls smashing a rival's nuclear ambitions," www.usatoday.com/news/world/2006-03-07-israel
   -osiraq_x.htm, accessed July 26, 2012.

5. Jeffrey Goldberg, "Israelis Grow Confident Strike on Iran's Nukes
   Can Work," *Bloomberg*, March 19, 2012, http://www.bloomberg.com/
   news/2012-03-19/israelis-grow-confident-strike-on-iran-s-nukes-can
   -work.html, accessed July 26, 2012.

6. Ronen Bergman, "Will Israel Attack Iran?" *The New York Times*,
   January 25, 2012, http://www.nytimes.com/2012/01/29/magazine/will
   -israel-attack-iran.html?_r=1&pagewanted=all, accessed July 26, 2012.

7. Elizabeth Bumiller, "Iran Raid Seen as Huge Task for Israeli Jets," *The
   New York Times*, February 19, 2012.

8. D.B. Grady, "If Israel Bombs Iran: Forecasting the Next 24 Hours,"
   The Week, March 19, 2012, http://theweek.com/bullpen/column
   /225737/if-israel-bombs-iran-forecasting-the-next-24-hours, accessed
   July 26, 2012.

9. Goldberg, "Israelis Grow Confident Strike on Iran's Nukes Can Work."

10. Mark Mazzetti and Thom Shanker, "U.S. War Game Sees Perils of
    Israeli Strike Against Iran," *The New York Times*, March 19, 2012, www
    .nytimes.com/2012/03/20/world/middleeast/united-states-war-game

11. Mazzetti and Shanker, "U.S. War Game Sees Perils of Israeli Strike
    Against Iran."

12. Gil Ronen, "War Game: Israeli Air Strike Deals Severe Blow to Iran
    Nukes," *Arutz Sheva*, April 17, 2012, www.israelnationalnews.com/
    News/News.aspx/154836, accessed July 26, 2012.

13. "Do Israeli-Azeri Ties Portend Conflict with Iran?" Guy Raz interview-
    ing Mark Perry on his article "Israel's Secret Staging Ground," *Foreign
    Policy* magazine, March 28, 2012, for *All Things Considered*, National
    Public Radio, April 1, 2012, http://www.npr.org/2012/04/01/14976
    1957/do-israeli-ties-portend-conflict-with-iran, accessed July 26, 2012.

14. "Khamenei: Israel is a cancerous tumor," *Jerusalem World News*, Feb-
    ruary 3, 2011, http://jerusalemworldnews.com/2012/02/03/
    khamenei-israel-is-a-cancerous-tumor.

15. Katz and Hendel, *Israel vs. Iran: The Shadow War*, 114.

16. "Iranian Details Plans to Annihilate Israel," *Israel My Glory*, May–June
    2012, 35.

17. Julian Borger, "Iran Warns Israel of 'Lightning' Reply to Any Attack, *The Guardian*, June 3, 2012, http://www.guardian.co.uk/world/2012/jun/03/iran-supreme-leader-israel-attack?newsfeed=true, accessed July 26, 2012.

18. Max Fisher, "Fear Itself: Americans Believe Iran Threat on Par with 1980s Soviet Union," *The Atlantic*, April 19 2012, http://www.theatlantic.com/international/archive/2012/04/fear-itself-americans-believe-iran-threat-on-par-with-1980s-soviet-union/256135, accessed July 26, 2012.

19. Fisher, "Fear Itself: Americans Believe Iran Threat on Par with 1980s Soviet Union."

20. Fisher, "Fear Itself: Americans Believe Iran Threat on Par with 1980s Soviet Union."

21. "Ahmadinejad: Iran's Nuke Program Like Train 'Without Brakes,'" Associated Press, February 25, 2007, http://www.foxnews.com/story/0,2933,254480,00.html, accessed July 26, 2012.

22. Kimberly Dozier, "Experts call Iran a major threat to U.S.," *The Daily Oklahoman*, February 1, 2012, 6A.

23. Dominic Tierney, "The Iran War Dial: Odds of Conflict Fall to 42%," *The Atlantic*, April 16, 2012, http://www.theatlantic.com/international/.../the-iran-war-dial-odds.../255943

24. "If the world wants to make the region insecure, we will make the world insecure: Iran threatens to shut Strait of Hormuz with military exercise," *Mail Online*, December 14, 2011 http://www.dailymail.co.uk/news/article-2073769, accessed July 26, 2012.

25. Con Coughlin, "Can Iran close down the Strait of Hormuz?" *The Telegraph*, January 5, 2012, http://www.telegraph.co.uk/news/worldnews/middleeast/iran/8995261/Can-Iran-close-down-the-Strait-of-Hormuz.html, accessed July 26, 2012.

26. Sri Jegarajah, "Iran Talks 'Will Fail'; Oil Risk Prevails: Roubini Analyst," *CNBC*, May 11, 2012, http://cnbc.com/id/47382551, accessed July 26, 2012.

27. Tony Capaccio, "Pentagon's Iran Buildup Call for Adding Laser Weapons," *Bloomberg*, March 19, 2012, http://www.bloomberg.com/news/2012-03-19/pentagon-s-iran-buildup-call-for-adding-laser-weapons.html, accessed July 26, 2012.

28. Arnaud de Borchgrave, "Slender geopolitical threads on Israel, Iran," *The Washington Times*, May 2, 2012, http://www.washingtontimes .com/news/2012/may/2/de-borchgrave-slender-geopolitical-threads

29. Katz and Hendel, *Israel vs. Iran: The Shadow War*, 167-87.

30. George Jahn, "Iran nuke work at bunker is confirmed," January 10, 2012, http://www.timesargus.com/article/20120110/ NEWS/701109997/0/OPINION01.

31. Rebecca Ann Stoil, "Barak: Qom Plant Immune to Regular Strike," *Jerusalem Post*, December 28, 2009.

32. Fredrik Dahl, "Iran has enough uranium for 5 bombs," *Reuters*, May 26, 2012, http://www.reuters.com/article/2012/05/26/us-nuclear-iran-uranium-idUSBRE84O0SN20120526, accessed July 26, 2012.

33. "Israel ambassador keeps door open to Iran strike," *CBS News*, March 15, 2012, http://www.cbsnews.com/8301-505263_162-57397940/ israel-ambassador-keeps-door-open-to-iran-strike, accessed July 26, 2012.

34. Fred Kaplan, "October Surprise: Why Israel May Feel Pressure to Attack Iran Before the U.S. Presidential Election," April 12, 2012, http://www.slate.com/articles/news_and_politics/war_stories/2012/04/nuclear_iran_why_i, accessed July 26, 2012.

35. This story from Barnhouse is related by James Montgomery Boice, *The Last and Future World* (Grand Rapids: Zondervan Publishing House, 1974), 49-50.

36. John F. Walvoord, *Armageddon, Oil and the Middle East Crisis: What the Bible Says About the Future of the Middle East and the End of Western Civilization*, rev. ed. (Grand Rapids: Zondervan, 1990), 27.

Chapter 2: Iran vs. Israel—from Shadow War to Showdown

1. Matthew Kroenig as quoted in Ronen Bergman, "Will Israel Attack Iran?," *The New York Times*, January 25, 2012, http://www.nytimes .com/2012/01/29/magazine/will-israel-attack-iran.html?page wanted=all, accessed July 26, 2012.

2. Benjamin Netanyahu as quoted in Dan Ephron, "If Israel Attacks Iran," *Newsweek*, October 15, 2012, 42.

3. Richard Stengel, "Bibi's Choice," *Time*, May 28, 2012, 35-36.

4. Yaakov Katz and Yoaz Hendel, *Israel vs. Iran: The Shadow War* (Washington, DC: Potomac Books, 2012), 9.

5. Reza Kahlili, "Iran committed to 'full annihilation of Israel,' says top Iranian military commander," *The Daily Caller*, May 20, 2012, http://news.yahoo.com/iran-committed-full annihilation-israel-says-top-iranian-033409439.html, accessed July 27, 2012.

6. Kahlili, "Iran committed to 'full annihilation of Israel,' says top Iranian military commander."

7. Mohammad Davari, "Iran oil sector hit by 'cyber attack,'" *Google News*, April 23, 2012 http://www.google.com/hostednews/afp/article/ALe qM5ivdP6nle_OuBNCj2NAL2rBVQ5-lQ?docId=CNG.a86eb6b27 01ce148592ac01588b748be.41, accessed July 27, 2012.

8. Mohammad Davari, "Iran oil sector hit by 'cyber attack.'"

9. Mohammad Davari, "Iran oil sector hit by 'cyber attack.'"

10. Lee Ferran, Alexander Marquardt and Colleen Curry, "Flame Cyber Attack: Israel Behind Largest Cyber Spy Weapon Ever?," *ABC News*, May 29, 2012, http://abcnews.go.com/Blotter/flame-cyber-attack -israel-largest-cyber-spy-weapon/story?id=16449339, accessed July 27, 2012.

11. Dave Reisinger, "U.S., Israel fired up Flame cyberattack, report says," CNET News, June 20, 2012, http://news.cnet.com/8301-1009_3 -57456764-83/u.s-israel-fired-up-flame-cyberattack-report-says, accessed July 27, 2012.

12. Ronen Bergman, "Will Israel Attack Iran?," *The New York Times*, January 25, 2012, http://www.nytimes.com/2012/01/29/magazine/will -israel-attack-iran.html?_r=1&pagewanted=all, accessed July 26, 2012.

13. Bergman, "Will Israel Attack Iran?"

14. Fred Kaplan, "October Surprise: Why Israel May Feel Pressure to Attack Iran Before the U.S. Presidential Election," April 12, 2012, http://www.slate.com/articles/news_and_politics/war _stories/2012/04/nuclear_iran_why_i

15. Bergman, "Will Israel Attack Iran?"

16. Arnaud de Borchgrave, "Slender geopolitical threads on Israel, Iran," *The Washington Times*, May 2, 2012, http://www.washingtontimes .com/news/2012/may/2/de-borchgrave-slender-geopolitical-threads

17. Jim Michaels, "Israeli attack on Iran would be complex operation," *USA Today*, Februrary 13, 2012, http://www.usatoday.com/news/world/story/2012-02-13/israel-iran-attack/53083160/1, accessed July 30, 2012.

18. Jim Michaels, "Israeli attack on Iran would be complex operation."

19. Mark Whittington, "Israel Would Be Justified in Launching a Strike Against Iran," Yahoo.com, June 5, 2012, http://news.yahoo.com/israel-justified-launching-strike-against-iran-214000414.html, accessed July 30, 2012.

20. "How will Israel attack Iran?" *Ynetnews.com*, November 9, 2011, http://www.ynetnews.com/articles/0,7340,L-4146086,00.html, accessed July 30, 2012.

21. Tia Goldenberg, "Israel gets fourth German submarine," Associated Press, *Bloomberg Businessweek.com*, May 3, 2012, http://www.businessweek.com/ap/2012-05/D9UHASP00.htm, accessed July 30, 2012.

22. Yoav Zitun, "Israel gets 4th German submarine," *Ynetnews.com*, May 3, 2012, http://www.ynetnews.com/articles/0,7340,L-4224486,00.html, accessed July 30, 2012.

23. Katz and Hendel, *Israel vs. Iran: The Shadow War*, 190.

Chapter 3: Show Me the Mahdi

1. Mortimer B. Zuckerman, "Moscow's Mad Gamble," *U.S. News and World Report*, January 30, 2006, Internet Edition.

2. Joel C. Rosenberg, "Iranian Defense Minister: War with Israel Means Twelfth Imam Is Coming," September 21, 2012, http://flashtrafficblog.wordpress.com/2012/09/21/iranian-defense-minister-war-with-israel means-twelfth-imam-is-coming/.

3. Reza Kahlili, "Iran committed to 'full annihilation of Israel,' says top Iranian military commander," *The Daily Caller*, May 20, 2012, http://news.yahoo.com/iran-committed-full annihilation-israel-says-top-iranian-033409439.html

4. Mahmoud Ahmadinejad, quoted in "Mahmoud Ahmadinejad in quotes," *The Telegraph*, June 10, 2012, http://www.telegraph.co.uk/news/worldnews/middleeast/iran/7816442/Mahmoud-Ahmadinejad-in-quotes.html, accessed July 27, 2012.

5. Ahmadinejad, quoted in "Ahmadinejad: the Era of Zionism is Over," *Jerusalem Post*, April 18, 2011, www.jpost.com/MiddleEast/Article .aspx?id=217081, accessed July 27, 2012.

6. Ahmadinejad, quoted by Islamic Republic News Agency, as reported in "Iranian leader: Wipe out Israel," *CNN.com*, October 27, 2005, http://edition.cnn.com/2005/WORLD/meast/10/26/ahmadinejad, accessed July 27, 2012.

7. Ahmadinejad, quoted in "Ahmadinejad: the Era of Zionism is Over."

8. Thomas Erdbrink, "Iran's Vice President Makes Anti-Semitic Speech at Conference," *The New York Times,* June 26, 2012, http://www.nytimes .com/2012/06/27/world/middleeast/irans-vice-president-rahimi -makes-anti-semitic-speech.html?_r=1&smid=tw-share, accessed July 26, 2012.

9. Anton La Guardia, "Divine Mission Driving Iran's New Leader," January 14, 2006, http://www.telegraph.co.uk/news/worldnews/ middleeast/iran/1507818/Divine-mission-driving-Irans-new-leader.html.

10. Thomas Erdbrink, "Ahmadinejad Criticized for Saying Long-Ago Imam Mahdi Leads Iran," *The Washington Post*, May 8, 2008, http:// www.washingtonpost.com/wp-dyn/content/article/2008/05/07/ AR2008050703587.html, accessed July 27, 2012.

11. Joel C. Rosenberg, "Why Iran's Top Leaders Believe That the End of Days Has Come," *FoxNews.com*, November 07, 2011, http://www .foxnews.com/opinion/2011/11/07/why-irans-top-leaders-believe-that -end-days-has-come, accessed July 27, 2012.

12. John Bolton, as quoted in Scott Keyes, "In Midst of Libya Conflict, Bolton Argues For New War In Iran: 'Got to Walk and Chew Gum at the Same Time,'" *Progressive News Daily*, March 26, 2011, http://www .progressivenewsdaily.com/?p=13839, accessed July 27, 2012.

13. Joel C. Rosenberg, "Understanding Egypt, the Twelfth Imam, and the End of Days," guest post on *The Blaze*, February 9, 2011, http://www .theblaze.com/blog/2011/02/09/understanding-egypt-the-twelfth -iman-and-the-end-of-days, accessed July 27, 2012.

14. Erick Stakelbeck, "Iranian Video Says Mahdi is 'Near,'" *CBN.com*, April 3, 2011, http://www.cbn.com/cbnnews/world/2011/March/ Iranian-Regime-Video-Says-Mahdi-is-Near, accessed July 27, 2012.

15. Ryan Mauro, "Iran's End Time Documentary," March 29, 2011, *Front PageMagazine.com*, http://www.frontpagemag.com/2011/03/29/iran's -end-times-documentary, accessed July 27, 2012.

16. Erick Stakelbeck, "Iranian Video Says Mahdi is 'Near'"; Jonathon M. Seidl, "'The Coming is Near': New Eerie Iran Propaganda Vid Trumpets Imminent Return of the 12th Imam," March 28, 2011, www.the blaze.com/stories/new-iran…vid…imminent-return-of-12th-imam -the-coming-is-near, accessed July 27, 2012.

17. Jonathon M. Seidl, "'The Coming is Near': New Eerie Iran Propaganda Vid Trumpets Imminent Return of the 12th Imam."

18. Jonathon M. Seidl, "'The Coming is Near': New Eerie Iran Propaganda Vid Trumpets Imminent Return of the 12th Imam."

19. Tim LaHaye, *Jesus: Why the World Is Still Fascinated by Him* (Colorado Springs, CO: David C. Cook, 2009), 43.

Chapter 4: Unleashing the Dogs of Terror

1. Chris Mitchell, "Winds of War: Will Israel Strike Iran Soon?," *CBN News*, May 1, 2012, www.charismanews.com/world/33320-winds-of -war-will-israel-strike, accessed July 27, 2012.

2. Ehud Barak, quoted in Yaakov Katz and Yoaz Hendel, *Israel vs. Iran: The Shadow War* (Washington, DC: Potomac Books, 2012), 193.

3. "Nasrallah tells Iran VP: Hezbollah ready for any challenge," *The Daily Star*, May 4, 2012, http://www.dailystar.com.lb/News/Poli tics/2012/May-04/172289-nasrallah-tells-iran-vp-hezbollah-ready-for -any-challenge.ashx, accessed July 27, 2012.

4. Military Intelligence Chief Major General Aviv Kochavi, whose estimate is reported by Amos Harel in "Some 200,000 missiles aimed consistently at Israel, top IDF officer says," *Haaretz*, February 2, 2012, http://www.haaretz.com/news/diplomacy-defense/some -200-000-missiles-aimed-consistently-at-israel-top-idf-officer -says-1.410584, accessed July 27, 2012.

5. Marcus George, "Iranian general: military strike would be the end of Israel," *Reuters*, June 23, 2012, http://www.reuters.com/arti cle/2012/06/23/us-iran-israel-threat-idUSBRE85M0C320120623, accessed July 27, 2012.

6. Jeffrey Goldberg, "Israelis Grow Confident Strike on Iran's Nukes

Can Work," *Bloomberg*, March 19, 2012, http://www.bloomberg.com/
news/2012-03-19/israelis-grow-confident-strike-on-iran-s-nukes-can
-work.html, accessed July 26, 2012.

7. Mark Mazzetti and Thom Shanker, "U.S. War Game Sees Perils of
Israeli Strike Against Iran," *The New York Times*, March 19, 2012, www
.nytimes.com/2012/03/20/world/middleeast/united-states-war-game.

8. Erika Solomon, "Hezbollah says able to strike anywhere in Israel,"
Reuters, May 11, 2012, http://www.reuters.com/article/2012/05/11/us
-hezbollah-israel-idUSBRE84A15420120511, accessed July 27, 2012.

9. Joel Leyden, "Hezbollah Iran Missiles Slam Hadera Israel—Nuclear
War Approaching?," *Israel News Agency*, August 5, http://www.israel
newsagency.com/haderaisraeliranrocketsnuclearwar4848070805.html,
accessed July 27, 2012.

10. Ronen Bergman, "Will Israel Attack Iran?," *The New York Times*, January 25, 2012, http://www.nytimes.com/2012/01/29/magazine/will
-israel-attack-iran.html?_r=1&pagewanted=all, accessed July 26, 2012.

11. See http://www.adl.org/main_Israel/hamas_facts.htm, accessed July
26, 2012.

12. See http://www.adl.org/main_Israel/hamas_facts.htm.

13. Enad Benari, "Hamas Won't Fight Israel Over Iran, Says Haniyeh,"
Arutz Sheva, May 11, 2012, http://www.Israelnationalnews.com/News/
News.aspx/155693, accessed July 27, 2012.

14. Mazzetti and Shanker, "U.S. War Game Sees Perils of Israeli Strike
Against Iran."

15. Benari, "Israel Warns Hizbullah Over Responding to Attack on Iran,"
Arutz Sheva, May 8, 2012, http://www.israelnationalnews.com/News/
News.aspx/155566.

16. Adrian Blomfield, "Israel warns Hizbollah over Iran," *The Telegraph*,
May 6, 2012, http://www.telegraph.co.uk/news/worldnews/middle
east/9249171/Israel-warn-Hizbollah-over-Iran.html, accessed July 27,
2012.

17. Bryanna Tidmarsh, "Israel deploys Iron Dome in Beersheba,"
Bellarmine Concord, March 30, 2011.

18. Yaakov Katz, "US to announce massive Iron Dome package," *The
Jerusalem Post*, May 13, 2012, http://www.jpost.com/Defense/Article
.aspx?id=269763, accessed July 27, 2012.

19. Luis Ramirez, "US Boosts Funding for Israel's 'Iron Dome' Defense System," *Voice of America*, May 17, 2012, http://www.voanews.com/content/us-boosts-funding-for-israel-iron-dome-defense-system/667202.html, accessed July 27, 2012.

20. See http://www.missilethreat.com/missiledefensesystems/id.10/system_detail.asp, accessed July 27, 2012.

Chapter 5: What Will Happen to America?

1. Glenn Beck, April 2009.

2. John F. Walvoord, *The Nations in Prophecy* (Grand Rapids: Zondervan Publishing House, 1967), 175.

3. Charles C. Ryrie, *The Best Is Yet to Come* (Chicago: Moody, 1981), 109-110.

4. *World*, March 22/29, 2008, 18. This statistic comes from a report by the Centers for Disease Control and Prevention.

5. David Klepper, "Gay-relationship debates at turning point?," Associated Press, in *The Daily Oklahoman*, May 29, 2011, 10A.

6. Jeffrey M. Jones, "Americans' Outlook for U.S. Morality Remains Bleak: Three-quarters say moral values in U.S. are getting worse," May 17, 2010, in *The Gallup Poll: Public Opinion 2010* (Lanham: Rowman & Littlefield Publishers, Inc., 2011), 162.

7. Michelle Schuman, "Is the Almighty Dollar Doomed?," *Time*, April 6, 2009, http://www.time.com/time/business/article/0,8599,1889588,00.html, accessed July 30, 2012.

8. Rich Miller and Simon Kennedy, "G-20 Shapes New World Order with Lesser Role for U.S. Markets," *Bloomberg*, April 3, 2009, http://www.bloomberg.com/apps/news?pid=newsarchive&sid=axEnb_LXw5yc, accessed July 30, 2012.

9. Nick Gillespie, "News Flash: Entitlement Spending Grows Like Giant Cancer on U.S. Economy," January 25, 2010, reason.com/blog/2010/01/25/news-flash-entitlement-spending, accessed July 30, 2012.

10. Niall Ferguson, "An Empire At Risk," *Newsweek*, December 7, 2009, 44.

11. Niall Ferguson, "An Empire At Risk," 44.

12. Niall Ferguson, "An Empire At Risk," 42, 44.

13. Niall Ferguson, "An Empire At Risk," 44.

14. Mona Charen, "Hardly a Friend to Israel," *The Daily Oklahoman*, May 25, 2011, 11.

15. Ben Feller, "Face to face, Netanyahu rejects Obama on borders," Associated Press, May 21, 2011, http://www.timesfreepress.com/news/2011/may/21/face-face-netanyahu-rejects-obama-borders, accessed July 30, 2012.

16. Mona Charen, "Hardly a Friend to Israel," 11.

Chapter 6: The Coming Middle East Peace

1. See http://www.brainyquote.com/quotes/authors/d/david_bengurion.html#cZ3uZ757SvsGBo4t.99, accessed July 30, 2012.

2. "Poll: More than half of Egyptians want to cancel peace treaty with Israel," The Associated Press, April 26, 2011, http://www.haaretz.com/news/diplomacy-defense/poll-more-than-half-of-egyptians-want-to-cancel-peace-treaty-with-israel-1.358107, accessed July 30, 2012.

3. This chart was also used in Mark Hitchcock, *2012, the Bible, and the End of the World* (Eugene, OR: Harvest House Publishers, 2009), 144.

4. Charles H. Dyer, *World News and Bible Prophecy* (Wheaton, IL: Tyndale House Publishers, 1995), 214.

Chapter 7: The Ezekiel Prophecy

1. John Mark Ruthven, *The Prophecy That Is Shaping History* (Fairfax, VA: Xulon Press, 2003), i.

2. Thomas Ice, "Ezekiel 38 and 39: Part II," www.pre-trib.org/data/pdf/Ice-(Part2)Ezekiel38&39.pdf, accessed July 30, 2012.

3. Josephus, *Antiquities* 1.6.1.

4. The Hebrew scholar Heinrich Friedrich Wilhelm Gesenius identified Rosh as Russia. See Heinrich Friedrich Wilhelm Gesenius, *Gesenius' Hebrew-Chaldee Lexicon to the Old Testament* (Grand Rapids: Eerdmans, 1949), 752. For an excellent presentation of the grammatical and philological support for taking Rosh as a place name, see James D. Price, "Rosh: An Ancient Land Known to Ezekiel," *Grace Theological Journal* 6 (1985): 67-89; Clyde E. Billington, Jr., "The Rosh People

in History and Prophecy (Part One)," *Michigan Theological Journal* 3 (1992): 55-64; Clyde E. Billington Jr., "The Rosh People in History and Prophecy (Part Two)" *Michigan Theological Journal* 3 (1992): 143-174; Clyde E. Billington Jr., "The Rosh People in History and Prophecy (Part Three)," *Michigan Theological Journal* 4 (1993): 39-62; Jon Mark Ruthven and Ihab Griess, *The Prophecy That Is Shaping History: New Research on Ezekiel's Vision of the End* (Longwood, FL: Xulon Press, 2003), 61-62.

5. General Jerry Boykin, Epicenter Conference, San Diego, April 4, 2009.

6. Thomas Ice, "The Battle between Russia, Iran and Israel," http://practicalspiritualwarfare.com/end-times-8.html.

7. Melik Kaylan, "Russia's Stake in Syria and Iran," March 18, 2012, *WSJ.com*, http://online.wsj.com/article/SB10001424052702304450004577277820529873332.html, accessed July 30, 2012.

8. "Russia denies war games report," June 19, 2012, http://www.upi.com/Top_News/World-News/2012/06/19/Iran-Russia-China-Syria-to-hold-drill/UPI-93751340106919/#ixzz1yFVH50Xn, accessed July 30, 2012.

9. "Bashir: Sharia law will be strengthened if South Sudan votes to secede," *The Christian Science Monitor*, http://www.csmonitor.com/World/Africa/Africa-Monitor/2010/1223/Bashir-Sharia-law-will-be, accessed July 30, 2012.

10. Maggie Michael, "Freed of Gadhafi, Libya's Instability Only Deepens," *The Daily Oklahoman*, March 4, 2012, 13A.

11. Josephus, *Antiquities* 1.6.1. Yamauchi provides a thorough description of the ancient Scythians. See Edwin M. Yamauchi, *Foes from the Northern Frontier* (Grand Rapids: Baker Book House, 1992), 64-109.

12. Arnold Fruchtenbaum, *The Footsteps of the Messiah: A Study of the Sequence of Prophetic Events*, rev. ed. (Tustin, CA: Ariel Ministries, 2003), 111-112.

13. Heinrich Friedrich Wilhelm Gesenius, *Gesenius' Hebrew-Chaldee Lexicon of the Old Testament* (Grand Rapids: Baker, 1979), 875.

14. Arnold Fruchtenbaum, *The Footsteps of the Messiah: A Study of the Sequence of Prophetic Events*, 111.

15. Arnold Fruchtenbaum, *The Footsteps of the Messiah: A Study of the Sequence of Prophetic Events*, 112.

Chapter 8: The Times of the Signs

1. John F. Walvoord, *The Nations in Prophecy* (Grand Rapids, MI: Zondervan Publishing House, 1967), 6.

2. These examples are taken from "Travel Humor," http://csswebs.com/ Humor/Travel.asp. Greg Laurie, *Signs of the Times* (Dana Point, CA: Kerygma Publishing, 2011), 21-22.

Chapter 9: Do Not Let Your Heart Be Troubled

1. Franklin Delano Roosevelt, quoted in James Montgomery Boice, *The Last and Future World* (Grand Rapids: Zondervan Publishing House, 1974), 1-2.

2. See "The Beauty of Humility," http://stmaryvalleybloom.org/homily -22sunday-c.html.

3. Charles Dyer, *World News and Bible Prophecy* (Wheaton, IL: Tyndale House Publishers, 1995), 270.

Appendix 1: The Persia Prophecies

1. Many contemporary scholars reject the unity of the book and Isaiah's authorship of this section of the prophecy. They believe it was written by someone other than Isaiah after Cyrus had already risen by power. For a concise defense of the unity of Isaiah, see Geoffrey W. Grogan, "Isaiah," in *The Expositor's Bible Commentary*, gen. ed. Frank E. Gaebelein, vol. 6 (Grand Rapids: Zondervan Publishing House, 1986), 6-11.

2. Alfred Martin, *Isaiah: The Salvation of Jehovah* (Chicago: Moody Press, 1956), 76-77.

The Middle East Is on Fire.
How Much Worse Will It Get?

Widespread revolutions. New powers rising. Bitter conflicts. Power plays over oil supplies. Aspirations for nuclear dominance. And a pall of uncertainty as to how it will all play out.

What is going on?

Middle East Burning helps make sense of the bewildering firestorms raging in the Arab-Israeli world. Author Mark Hitchcock brings together historical context, today's headlines, and future Bible prophecies to provide clarity and answers to these questions and more:

- What's causing all the unrest in the Arab world?

- What's next for Egypt, Syria, and Libya?

- How are today's events connected with end-time prophecies?

- Are we on the brink of a nuclear holocaust?

- What role will America have in the last days?

A riveting and timely survey of things now and things to come!